LIGHT AIRS … EEZES

– A VICTORIAN NAVAL LIFE STORY –

With best wishes
Richard Bickford
xi.96.

– Richard F. Bickford –

LIGHT AIRS AND GENTLE BREEZES

– A VICTORIAN NAVAL LIFE STORY –

SIGN AT THE BICKFORD ARMS

TARTAN EDGE **SOUTH WEST SCOTLAND**

First Published in 1996

by

TARTAN EDGE
Gerrichrew, Mainsriddle
DUMFRIES
South West Scotland

Printed in Scotland by

Alba Printers Ltd.
Dumfries

ISBN 0 9521750 1 0

BRITISH LIBRARY CATALOGUING-IN-PUBLICATION DATA
A catalogue record for this book is available from the British Library

Cover design by:
Richard F. Bickford

By the same author 1993:

"The Story of John Paul Jones 1747-1792
a father of the United States Navy"

CONTENTS

LIGHT AIRS AND GENTLE BREEZES

- A VICTORIAN NAVAL LIFE STORY -

ILLUSTRATIONS

ACKNOWLEDGEMENTS

My grateful thanks in the preparation of this book are due to:-

Graham Salt of Naval Research Services for the very great help given in research and proof reading; without his interest this book would never have been written.

Both the Devon and Cornwall Family History Societies for their help with West Country matters.

Alanna Knight, an authority on Robert Louis Stevenson, for the supply of photograph and notes.

Ernest Mehew, author concerned with the publication of Robert Louis Stevenson letters, for invaluable advice in respect of the life of RLS in Samoa.

The Devon County Library for much helpful information.

John F. Lavelle B.A. for assistance with West Country research.

The National Maritime Museum, London for photographs of Naval vessels, and for help from The Royal Naval Museum, Portsmouth.

The National Trust, Exeter, for help with information on Dunsland House.

The Public Records Office for provision of copy documents.

British Columbia Archives and Records Service for provision of copy historical documents.

The Canadian Office of National Defence for assistance with information on Esquimalt Naval Base, B.C. Canada, and for help from Tony Holden.

Nicola Bickford for her work in the laborious task of typesetting the text.

The Bickford family for proof reading and Alba Printers Ltd for their help with production.

TO A LONG SUFFERING WIFE

AND FAMILY

4.am “Daylight, observed the wreck of NISERO on port beam and Dutch gunboat BEUCOULIU at anchor.

Temperature 65 degrees and PEGASUS making way at three knots in light airs.”

From log of H.M.S. PEGASUS
off the coast of Sumatra
19th February 1884.

PREFACE

When making a close assessment of the life and times of a character from the past there is often a tendency to drift away from the prime objective especially when distractions are numerous.

From a writers point of view any deflection from the prime topic should be resisted and concentration on the principal issue has to be maintained if a proper appreciation of the subject matter is to be achieved.

However, in this case conditions are a little different because considerations of family history are involved and in some cases there is an overlap of detail; accordingly it affords a special opportunity to offer something beyond an overall account of events that occurred over a particular span of time.

Because of the scope of the research undertaken in the course of assembling material for this book, it seems wasteful not to set down some information in respect of earlier generations of the Bickford family who lived in, or had early connections with, the West Country.

From Saxon times, the name of Bickford has been spelt in different ways appearing variously as Bickeford, Bicheford, Bykeford and Bikeford etc. The family originates in the main from Devonshire and Cornwall and has occupied lands in both Counties over the centuries.

When the Normans made grants of land they often named themselves after the place concerned. In those days Bighe or Biche signified 'little' and 'fordh' or 'vor' meant way, passage or ford; thus the name, Bickford, was constructed.

The old Saxon or Norman word 'tun' meaning 'enclosure' could be added to a place name which reveals that the 'tun' of Bikefortun probably signified a little ford with an enclosure consequently becoming 'Bickford town', which was situated at Plymton St. Mary in South Devon.

The Manor of Bike, was held in Saxon times by Eldred, the King's forester, who was responsible for collecting the King's dues and later by Robert le

Bastard at the time of the Devon Domesday in 1085/6 which makes reference to Bickforda.

Early Tax Rolls and the Tester de Nevill show that Ralph de Bikeford held Bikeford town in 1241, William de Bikeford in 1285 and 1303; John de Bikeford held it in 1345.

There appears to have been a Sir William Bikeford who was a supporter of Richard III and according to Knight 'fees' he was killed at the Battle of Bosworth. Understandably, there is a gap before subsequent references are made in 1565 when Nicholas Bikeford was Mayor of Plymouth and John Bikeford was involved in the perambulation of Dartmouth in 1608; it is noted that John leased the Manor of Woolhouse and West Alwynton in South Devon and his son bought it in 1625.

The register of Plymton St. Mary indicates that there were Bickfords residing at Bickford town in 1675; the property there subsequently passing from Bickford to the families of Crocker and then Avant.

Devonshire is the second largest County in Britain. The northern area is the most inaccessible, the middle mainly consists of moorland, while the south includes market towns and a coast of cliffs and shore where there are now holiday resorts and a number of fishing ports; in addition there is a substantial Naval dockyard at Devonport together with other naval establishments.

The northern districts of Dartmoor are skirted by land which is relatively poor and infertile by comparison with the rich red soil of South Devon. It is a remote area with long established small sleepy villages and hidden farms, making change slow and communication awkward by way of deep sided lanes. The restricted movement of the inhabitants has resulted in frequent inter-marriage, making for a large number of near family connections.

In former times major properties were seldom to be found in this part of the country so, for travellers to encounter a substantial house in this kind of landscape, would have been a surprise in the extreme, especially if they had only come across an occasional Inn or windmill.

However, it was in this northern region of the County, in the 17th Century, that the Bickford family was established at Dunsland House in the Parish of Bradford in North Devon by way of the fortuitous marriage of William Bickford to Grace Arscott in 1634; she was an heiress, who had inherited the property.

The Squire invariably became the local Magistrate, hence the Justice Room in the House, and he had to rely upon his poor land and low rents for income. These conditions restricted the development of many a fine house and so, much depended upon inheritance and/or a beneficial marriage to bring in the necessary funds; the occupation of properties by several generations of one family often bear witness to this method of retention and maintenance.

In due course Grace gave birth to a son named Arscott who in turn married, as his third wife, Briget Prideaux, the daughter of Edmund Prideaux of Place, near Padstow in Cornwall, in 1683; it is from their second son, Edmund, a Barrister and a JP for Cornwall, who died in 1732, that the subject of this book always derived his line of relationship, though it was somewhat tenuous.

Family inheritance is usually by way of the eldest son, though not always, as was the case of Bickford v. Hoblyn which concerned a wife's inheritance and ownership of considerable lands in Cornwall. The legal case was eventually taken to The House of Lords in 1724 where a previous judgement was overturned in favour of the appellants, William and Damaris Bickford.

Interestingly enough, the first action in this case, which took place before The Master of the Rolls, was given in favour of the Bickfords; this was subsequently reversed by The Lord Chancellor, The Earl of Macclesfield (who by coincidence was an early relative of the author of this book, on his mother's side), before going to the Lords.

It seems to have been worth while spending these few moments to take a glance at the background to the family although it must be said that because descent of Admiral Bickford is by way of a second son, about whom little appears to have been recorded, it has made for some difficulties in substantiating early lineage. However, 'Visitations of Devon' by Vivian provides an invaluable and detailed pedigree for the early Bickfords, dating from 1600; a copy of this document is included as Appendix II.

Among other matters, Vivian's record shows a connection with the Parkers of Saltram House at Plymton because of Arscott Bickford's marriage to Mary Parker (as his first wife) in 1660; a television programme was made by the B.B.C. in 1969 about the Parker family which they followed up with a book. Saltram House is now the Headquarters of The National Trust in the West Country.

It is also notable that many Bickfords emigrated and settled in the United States, Canada and Australia in the 18th and 19th Centuries. It is said that an early community was established on the St Clair River in Michigan, U.S.A. and to this day there are a number of geographical features named after the family in British Columbia, Canada.

We are brought into the 20th Century by linking the Vivian pedigree with the notes of Lieutenant Colonel Bickford, the Admiral's brother (my great Uncle), who was particularly interested in the subject of family history.

These notes have an additional interest of their own in as much as they formed some background to the information provided by the first National Trust guidebook to Dunsland, which was produced as a memorial to the house following its destruction by fire in 1967, and has since been reprinted.

Delving into the past by way of family history is a fascinating occupation and can become obsessive when one find leads to another and so on. It is no surprise, therefore, to find how many people both young and old are joining the various family history societies established all over Britain; the growing number of searchers to be encountered at the many Record Offices is an indication of the interest being shown in the subject.

The opening Chapter of this book briefly refers to the sad destruction of Dunsland House and to the generations of Bickford's who occupied it over a period, many of whom lie buried at the little church at Bradford nearby. A list of the owners of the house is provided at the end of this volume.

Following upon the foregoing it must be stressed that this book is primarily concerned with the life of a Victorian sailor and of his near antecedents.

It was prompted in the first place by the gift, some years ago, of a broken ditty-box, which had belonged to my Grandfather, Admiral A.K. Bickford C.M.G.

More recently the box was found to contain some literary treasure; among material of little consequence there was a batch of correspondence, Naval Appointments and Letters of Commendation; all of immense interest.

Up to this time all detail of the Admiral's life available to me had been confined to a newspaper cutting of his Obituary published in The Times of 11th October 1927 noting his 50 years service in the Royal Navy. In my early years I had gleaned some odd pieces of information about him from my father and from members of the family but in truth they did not mean a great deal to me at the time.

However, as these acquired papers provided a background to the life of a prominent member of the family, they inspired me to find out more. My wife and family subsequently encouraged me to commit the facts to paper; having embarked on a period of research, and given the enormous help of Graham Salt, an expert on Victorian Naval History, I have since been able to assemble the pieces of a jigsaw which have revealed more than I had ever hoped.

They concern a life of substantial interest to me and perhaps others; accordingly the tale is now told.

I would, however, ask readers of the pages which follow to accept my apologies for the omission of anyone of interest who should have been included and also for any inadvertent inaccuracies in the content of what is, in many respects, a family book.

R.F.B. Scotland 1996

Dunsland House

(With permission of the National Trust)

CHAPTER I

A LADDER OF PROGRESS

On the moors of North Devon in a remote position, a little way off the road joining Holsworthy with Hatherleigh, lies the site of Dunsland House.

A mile or so distant stands The Bickford Arms , providing locals and travellers alike with sustenance for their journeys.

On the night of 17th November 1967 as the customers left the bar of the Inn they noticed a glow in the night sky and there was a smell of smoke in the air. The "Big house" of Dunsland was alight and few hours later nothing remained but the smoking ruins of a great stone mansion dating from Tudor times which had been passed down to succeeding generations through inheritance; it had been cared for by the National Trust since 1954 and they had furnished it with precious items - all had been destroyed.

The Bickfords had been the owners of Dunsland from 1686 to 1817 and it was from Edmund, the second son of Arscott Bickford, who died in 1693, and his third wife Briget Prideaux that the principal character of this story claimed descent.

Some generations later, on 11th August 1844 in Madras, India, the birth of Andrew Kennedy Bickford was recorded.

His father, William, was Master and owner of the barque 'WORCESTER' of 521 tons; quite a sizable vessel for those days. She was built in Hull and registered in London, regularly sailing between London and Madras prior to 1849, according to Lloyds Register of Shipping, probably in support of the East India Company.

In 1841 he married Andrew's mother Maria Pinnock Kennedy, at Stoke Damerel, Devonport. Her father, Captain Kennedy Royal Navy had enjoyed a colourful naval career world wide, and in turn his father before him, originating from Ayrshire in the West of Scotland, had been a mariner of fifty-five years standing.

On the Bickford side there is evidence that Andrew's grandfather, Joseph, was a miller in the 1780's owning a tidal mill in the Parish of Maker in Cornwall just over the water from Devonport. Tidal mills were devised in historical times; they were constructed on estuaries or creeks and operated by a controlled rush of sea water, from very large tidal mill pools or small lakes, which drove the mill wheels. Sometimes jetties and piers were built nearby to accommodate moderate sized sailing ships engaged in the grain trade.

Andrew Kennedy Bickford, though born in India did not spend long there. First of all his mother died in 1846, possibly of fever, at Royapooram in the Principality of Madras where there was a family home and then his father appears to have died at sea shortly afterwards, on his way home.

There were three children of the marriage. First William, then Andrew and finally Maria, who was born at sea.

After the death of their parents, when William was barely four years old and the other two mere infants, all three were brought back to England in the charge of an aunt, a Miss Marianne Kennedy, an elder sister of their mother.

Andrew and his sister were sent to live with their maternal grandfather, Captain Kennedy Royal Navy, at Tamar Terrace, Stoke Damerel, Devonport while the eldest boy, William, joined his paternal grandfather, Joseph, at Newport House in the Parish of Stonehouse between Plymouth and Devonport.

William, in due course, joined the Royal Marine Artillery eventually passing into the Staff College at Greenwich; he served in the first Ashanti Campaign of 1870 and rose to the rank of Lieutenant Colonel.

Andrew was sent to school at Foster's, Stubbington where he secured a good basic education and seems to have done well.

A naval career was the logical profession for the lad after having lived during his early years with his grandfather, Captain Kennedy. Moreover he had listened to tales of the sea and been told of his father's exploits in East Indiamen; it was no coincidence that the house they occupied was situated near the naval quarter of Devonport where sailors and their families were always about.

In many households it was felt that by tradition at least one son would enter the Royal Navy and go to sea in spite of the dangers and discomforts it invariably involved.

Accordingly, at the age of thirteen Andrew managed to secure a 'nomination' for entry into the Service, probably with the assistance of his grandfather's friends.

In those days, before the introduction of training in 'BRITANNIA', [1] 'Osborne', and later in 1903, when there was entry to R.N. College Dartmouth by competitive examination, potential cadets, after securing a nomination, usually from someone connected with the Navy, applied for entry and acceptance; the next step was the passing of an oral examination followed by a medical test.

With his naval background, Andrew Kennedy Bickford overcame these hurdles without too much difficulty early in 1858 and thus began a career spanning fifty years of service to his country.

His sister, Maria, meanwhile remained at home and some years later married a young naval officer, Shalto Douglas, who enjoyed a distinguished

1. The home of Queen Victoria in Isle of White where she died 1901; used as Naval officers training establishment 1903 - 1921 in conjunction with R.N. College, Dartmouth.

career in the service and eventually retired as a well decorated Admiral; two of his three sons were also commissioned in the Royal Navy.

Initially, Andrew had to visit the naval tailor to be measured for his uniform; always a significant occasion. When a cadet in the Royal Navy donned his first smart reefer jacket with its brass buttons and put on his serge trousers, it represented an important step in the process of growing up in a man's world.

Captain Kennedy did not have a great deal of money so his grandson's future was something of financial concern. Although it was not always the case, parents often started off their sons as cadets or midshipmen with a private allowance of £40 or £50 a year against which the captain endorsed quarterly bills drawn by the youngsters. As he himself became financially liable he usually insisted that the money should be deposited with his Agent ashore and then the quarterly bills of £10 were drawn on the Agent.

As mess bills for wine, a servant, washing, extras and pocket money all had to be accounted for over a period of three months by boys of thirteen and fourteen, it is not surprising that they frequently became insolvent. In that event it was with embarrassment they had to leave the mess and eat ship's provisions over their sea chests elsewhere. Later on when it was considered that these arrangements were unsatisfactory, payment by parents was made directly to the Paymaster and he paid the mess bills and handed any surplus, as pocket money, to the young men.

After all the family excitement was over, young Bickford's first journey was to Portsmouth to join the initial training ship H.M.S. ILLUSTRIOUS on 6th March 1858. She was a hulk used as both a guard ship and a harbour training ship where cadets would study mathematics, navigation, French and seamanship.

It was a tough time for Andrew as a naval cadet during the training period. For lads of the tender age of about fourteen a great deal was demanded of them with a life that was both vigorous and the discipline strict. It is said that either for initiation or disobedience the punishment was to have the bridge of the nose slit and pepper and salt applied to the wound; whether

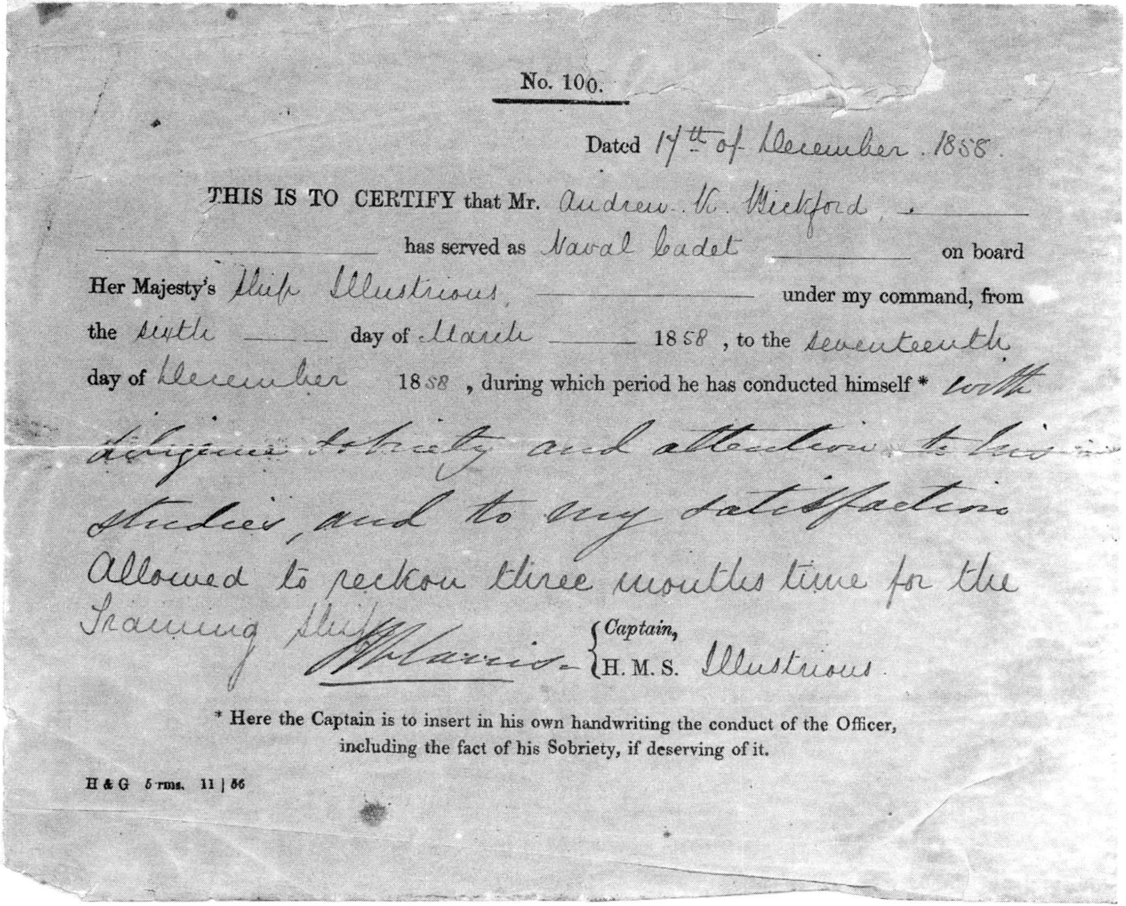
No. 100.

Dated 17th of December. 1858.

THIS IS TO CERTIFY that Mr. Andrew K. Bickford, has served as Naval Cadet on board Her Majesty's Ship Illustrious under my command, from the sixth day of March 1858, to the seventeenth day of December 1858, during which period he has conducted himself * with diligence, sobriety and attention to his studies, and to my satisfaction. Allowed to reckon three months time for the Training Ship

R. Harris, Captain, H. M. S. Illustrious

* Here the Captain is to insert in his own handwriting the conduct of the Officer, including the fact of his Sobriety, if deserving of it.

H & G 5 rms. 11 | 56

First Naval Report on Cadet A.K. Bickford R.N., 1858

this was done officially or otherwise is not recorded. Anyhow this was the kind of treatment that young boy cadets had to endure; Andrew was one of them.

Life at sea was never easy and it was considered that a harsh beginning was the way to prepare for it. Having survived such hardships for ten months, Andrew passed out with a certificate from the Captain of H.M.S. ILLUSTRIOUS stating that he had conducted himself "with diligence, sobriety and attention to his studies, and to my satisfaction"; this gained him three months seniority after proceeding to the sail training ship H.M.S. LIFFEY where he did some sea time and where he remained from the end of 1858 until March 1862. She was a 51 gun wooden, screw frigate, of 2654 tons with a telescopic funnel. She did good service and ended her days on the South American coast as a store ship and she was finally sold in 1903.

On leaving the ship his report was equally commendable and he was shortly made up to midshipman. He proudly put on his new uniform jacket with its white patches to indicate his rank, having obtained a First Class Certificate which stated that he had passed "a good examination".

Midshipmen had to sling their hammocks over their sea chests in the 'cockpit' in the lower part of the ship or in the Gunroom, where they were allocated quarters in this partitioned after-section of the lower deck which usually contained two guns. In the event of action the partitions were removed and the two guns, one on either side, were run out in line with the others.

The duties of these young men were varied, and apart from watch-keeping and the writing up of the log, which was often found difficult as the senior officers were very particular in this regard, their other tasks included working at speed aloft in the rigging, completing such operations as striking lower yards and topmasts to reduce wind pressure; sometimes there was competition between ships and between the midshipmen themselves in such work.

Additionally their education included learning to box-the-compass, navigation, sail-making with rope work, gun drill, taking charge of boats and learning to give orders. When the ship cleared for action one of their jobs was to ensure that all hammocks were moved to the netting on deck where they were used for protection.

Few of the new entrants were bullied by the older boys although frightening tales were related to them and they had practical jokes played on them such as being told to find something in the 'Fog locker' or even to 'Ask the Purser's Steward to be measured for a Spoon'!

Because these very young raw officers were somewhat ignorant of the language and ways of the sea they had to learn quickly if they were to survive the rigours of daily life and certainly they lived in some awe of their senior officers who paced the decks in their smart frock coats.

One of the other duties they had to perform was to turn up to witness punishment which was never a popular ordeal as it usually involved a flogging for the charge of insubordination, fighting or desertion. The officers, wearing swords, and the ships company had to attend, while the Marines, bearing side arms, also had to be present; when the 'Cat' or 'Cat o' nine tails' (a rope's end with unwound strands and knotted ends) was applied it was a messy and gruesome affair.

As for the making up of crews of vessels in the early days when there was no continuous service; after a ship had completed a commission of three to five years, she was 'paid off' and the crew went on leave. Another ship was then sought on a voluntary basis hence the saying 'one volunteer is better than ten pressed men'.

There were placards at sea ports inviting men to join with the enticement of a bounty. Recruiting stations were designated 'Rendezvous' and when a ship had a good reputation she was known as a 'happy ship' and there was less difficulty in drawing a crew. If more than one ship was concerned there was competition between them for crews. The first men joining had to do the initial heavy work so some joined later to avoid these tasks. There was, however, some pride in being amongst the 'first hundred' on the books.

When a recently constructed ship was involved it sometimes took months to

H.M.S. Liffey c. 1860
(By permission of the National Maritime Museum, London)

collect a crew especially if she was 'fitting out' which meant that she was a shell to start with, then towed into the harbour where her masts were stepped, she was rigged, and iron fresh-water tanks loaded into her bilges to act as ballast; a gallon of water a day was the crew's allowance and that included washing. As for food at sea, it was pretty basic and included meat pickled in brine, hard ships biscuit and potatoes, but seldom fresh vegetables. The diet was often supplemented with helpings of 'duff'; a grey coloured steamed pudding mixture. A tot of rum was the daily ration - when water was added it became 'grog' which would not keep and so prevented hoarding; it was nicknamed after the grogram material of the cloak worn by Admiral Vernon who introduced the procedure in 1740 to prevent drunkenness on board ships.

In September 1863, amid this atmosphere, Andrew was appointed to Her Majesty's Steam Ship 'BARROSA' as a midshipman. The specific mention that she was propelled by steam, on the Captain's report, was made because the Admiralty at that time was only beginning to accept the benefits of steam and ships often retained masts and sail, using steam only for manoeuvring in harbour. However for a time there were experiments in the use of "lifting screws" which could be lowered to support sail power when necessary; conversely the order 'up screw down funnel' was given when sail was being used to economise in coal usage, particularly on long patrols.

It was stated that while in 'BARROSA', Midshipman Bickford had constant charge of a watch at sea and was found to be "a zealous and promising young officer."

While still serving in her he was made up to Acting Sub-Lieutenant and the Captain again commended him to the extent of saying that he would willingly take Mr. Bickford as a Lieutenant in any ship he might Command - quite a compliment for a young officer but nonetheless a reward for obvious hard work.

From August 1863 to June 1864 'BARROSA' was in Yokohama as a member of a multi-national naval force of six ships from France, Holland and Britain which was ordered to force the Straits of Shimonoseki because of rebellion and violation of Treaties. In September a bombardment of the forts guarding the Straits was conducted for one and a half hours daily over four days. On the fifth day marines landed, the forts surrendered, and the ships returned to Yokohama. On 18th October Acting Sub-Lieutenant Bickford was transferred to H.M.S. EURYLUS, the flagship, in which he took passage home and he was again commended as "a very promising officer."

It seemed to Andrew that now was the time to decide on the future direction of his career if he was to succeed in terms of promotion.

His choice was to specialise in Gunnery and in this he was very foresighted. Apart from anything else, success in this department led to quicker advancement, besides which, it carried a specialist allowance at a time when money was particularly short for young officers.

Guns at that time were developing fast along with ship construction which was changing from timber and sail, to ironclad with steam propulsion.

In naval gunnery great advances had been made since the days of Trafalgar when Nelson's guns fired cannon balls varying in size from that of a billiard ball of 32 lbs to one the size of a football weighing 304 lbs; the former had a range of approximately 3000 yards but when firing the latter a gunner would be fortunate to achieve half that distance.

Progress was made rapidly and the range of guns increased enormously with the introduction of the French "Shell gun", which the Royal Navy came to adopt with some initial reluctance and only after it had been tested in the Crimea by the Russians against the Turkish Fleet with great success. It was the turning point in naval warfare because the fabric of a ships hull had to be altered to neutralise the revolution in gun construction with rifled barrels and explosive shells.

Within this context the British Armstrong gun of 1858 was produced; initially it was hazardous in the extreme owing to an imperfect fuse and there were many accidents when firing it. Only after a breech block and rifled barrel to control the flight of the shell had been perfected, was this kind of weapon more generally accepted.

The French had already realised that changes were demanded in ship construction to counteract gun development, and this was demonstrated when they built "LA GLOIRE" in 1859, a wooden hulled ironclad. The Admiralty, a year later in 1860, then constructed the first iron hulled ironclad, H.M.S. WARRIOR, to give protection against shells of the time. From then on developments became more sophisticated with turrets and batteries of guns, but this began rather disastrously in 1870 when H.M.S. CAPTAIN, with masts and a double deck construction, the lower one providing open observation for revolving turrets, capsized off Spain. Already papers had been written on the dangers of carrying sail on low freeboard ships and this accident lead to the abandonment of masts and sail and the introduction of gun turrets fore and aft for stability, supported by steam engines for propulsion.

It is worth explaining that steam power which had been invented in 1769 was only now being applied to ships in practical terms; it took until 1815, the year of the Battle of Waterloo, for a steam vessel to make her way from Greenock in Scotland to London in the South. This new form of propulsion for ships was not of immediate interest to the Admiralty who nicknamed the vessels "Smoke Jacks" and it was the Merchant Marine who were the real pioneers. However, in due course the advantages were recognised and paddle vessels were developed principally as naval tugs because as fighting ships they were considered to be too fragile.

Then came the propeller as an alternative. In 1842 two similar ships were provided by the navy as a test-bed; one, the 'RATTLER', was fitted with a screw and the other 'ALECTO' with paddle wheels. They were positioned stern to stern and a tug-of -war between them was carried out. Needless to say 'RATTLER' won the contest easily and there was no turning back to the old ways.

With steam and the introduction of ironclads there was a huge difference in speed in all weathers for such vessels when compared with sail. Additionally, the manoeuvrability of such ships made the firing of broadsides in line abreast obsolete; line ahead made for smaller targets and when swivel guns became available seamanship and tactics had to be completely revised.

The great Naval debate of the second half of the 19th and early 20th

Century took place between the supporters of the reliance on speed and less armament for warships of all classes, as against those advocating very powerful guns in more heavily armoured ships. The former view led to the construction, in the more modern context of the, less heavily armoured but faster, battle cruiser, such as H.M.S. HOOD in the 1920's, while earlier a number of battle cruisers had already been involved in the Battle of Jutland.

In the case for heavier guns and ships, the adherents to their argument got their way to some extent in 1908 (the year of Admiral Bickford's eventual retirement) when H.M.S. DREADNAUGHT was constructed with its monster guns in pairs, in five turrets, four of which, could be fired as a broadside; a number of heavy battleships of the 'R' Class such as 'RESOLUTION' and 'RAMILLIES' etc., were to follow so that to some extent, both sides of the argument got their way.

In later years there followed a further debate on the usage of coal versus oil as fuel for ships; the supporters for coal took the line that there was an unlimited worldwide supply of the material and coal bunkers in ships provided an additional line of protection while those in favour of oil stressed its convenience in usage and its extra efficiency as source of energy for the propulsion of ships.

All these matters had, in addition, to take into account developments which were occuring in related fields of naval warfare.

Arising out of the use of mines which had been available for many decades past, there came the self-propelled mine driven by compressed air, invented by Robert Whitehead in the mid 1860's. These under water projectiles were named 'torpedoes' and fast light craft, or Torpedo Boats (T.B.'s) were built to carry and launch them; the initial defence of a ship against torpedo attack was by way of steel nets attached to her hull but they were of limited value as a cutter attached to the torpedo was then devised to penetrate this barrier.

However, the torpedo, as an offensive weapon, eventually led to the building of the submarine which itself has become the ultimate under-water weapon when armed with torpedoes and sometimes a gun; even a seaplane for spotting work was once carried experimentally by both British and French

H.M.S. Renoun off Malta c. 1860
A 91 gun second Rate warship, powered by sail and steam
(from an early print)

submarines in the 1930's. These vessels were the forerunners of the modern nuclear submarine.

There had to be some defence against early Torpedo Boats so the Torpedo Boat Destroyer (T.B.D.) was introduced; it was a very fast, well armed craft with quick firing guns capable of discharging twelve rounds a minute thus it could easily destroy a torpedo boat. This vessel was the precursor of the modern destroyer which, in addition to providing a defensive screen for capital ships, now operates as a ship in its own right with an immense concentration of fire-power.

From 1860, when H.M.S. WARRIOR was built, to the turn of the century, Britain was a spectator to various wars to which she was not a party; thus the Admiralty could see from a distance the possibilities of constructing battleships of a totally new kind.

Such matters must have been appreciated by an ambitious young officer like Andrew Bickford, and the progress being made must have been an obvious encouragement for him to proceed with a career which involved intensive training in gunnery when not undertaking appointments at sea.

On his arrival back in England, after his Far Eastern experience, and to satisfy his enthusiasm, Acting Sub-Lieutenant Bickford was sent on "courses" at H.M.S. EXCELLENT, the gunnery school ship moored in Portsmouth harbour.

Subsequently, the gunnery school, H.M.S. EXCELLENT, was built ashore; originally there were two mud flats in Portsmouth harbour known as 'Whaley' and it is said that when the Royal Navy became interested in using them for rifle drill and field training in the early 1850's, the term 'Whale Island' was adopted in a desire to 'improve ones address'.

In the course of the development of the site, about 1500 convicts were used as a labour force to transport spoil to the site from the dockyard extensions and further dry docks, about a mile away; they were under the orders of warrant officers who had been trained to act as foremen by the garrison of the Royal Engineers. In 1890 levelling and drainage was put in hand prior to the construction of accommodation.

Very high standards were set for officers attending gunnery courses and passing out well could make a great difference to a career. Gunnery officers were the elite of the Navy.

The essential ingredients for success were enthusiastic keenness, pride in gunnery, strict discipline and the observance of meticulous smartness in appearance and at drill.

In October 1865 Andrew Bickford secured a Second Class passing out certificate from H.M.S. EXCELLENT, having obtained 250 marks out of 280, which shows the high standard expected and represented a good result.

In December of that year, now promoted to Lieutenant, he joined H.M.S. RESEARCH and with that ship he spent two years patrolling the coast of Ireland and visiting various Irish ports during the Fenian Riots. The Fenians were Irishmen who had returned from service in the American Civil War and were demonstrating their strong independent and nationalist feelings.

It was about that time that Lieutenant Bickford was given permission to marry. In Queenstown, Ireland, he met a pretty Irish girl of seventeen and the story goes that having seen her once he said he intended to marry her. Her name was Kathleen Louise Dore, the daughter of a local G.P., Dr Patrick Edward Dore, whose brother-in-law, as a matter of interest, was Maurice Power, Member of Parliament for the County of Cork at the time of Queen Victoria's first visit to Queenstown and who was, at one time, Governor of St. Lucia, in the West Indies.

After his marriage in 1868, Andrew brought Kathleen back to Southsea, by Portsmouth, where over subsequent years, they raised a family of five sons and two daughters, which included the author's father, 'Jack'.

Dr Dore died in 1881 on a journey from Ireland to New York to visit relatives. One evening on the Mail steamer he slipped and fell down the companion way and died two days later.

For young Bickford there followed more courses at H.M.S. EXCELLENT and for a period he was lent to H.M.S. TRAFALGAR, in the Squadron of Reserve, as Gunnery Officer, to smarten up the ship. His next appointment was as Gunnery Lieutenant in H.M.S. HECTOR in the spring of 1870.

Now as an experienced and efficient officer, an appointment to H.M.S. ACHILLIES was made in 1871 to superintend the drill of the Reserves and of the ships company. The promotional ladder was being climbed in text book manner.

He returned home after this term of duty, for a short period and then joined H.M.S. TOPAZE, a screw sailing frigate of 31 guns, as Gunnery Officer where he remained until November 1873.

The following year, after all the training and effort, it was now that real advancement took place with the appointment as First Lieutenant and Second in Command of H.M.S. AMETHYST, a corvette of 1970 tons armed with fourteen 6.3 inch muzzle loading guns.

He was now entering a critical period when, after ten or twelve years as a fully qualified Lieutenant, promotion to the rank of Commander was awaited with some trepidation; it is sometimes known as securing ones 'Brass Hat' because of the oak leaves on the peak of the cap worn by a Commander.

This represented perhaps the most important stage in his career for without this particular promotion it was impossible to achieve progress to the top echelons of the Service. Many have failed the test and have been 'passed over' to the extent that the navy, because of the system, has probably lost a good number of talented but unrecognised men.

Fortunately for Lieutenant Bickford, during his time in 'AMETHYST', he took part in a successful operation involving the eleven year old rebel ironclad turret ship 'HUASCAR' of 1100 tons which had been built by Lairds; she was armed with two 300 pounder guns. The action took place in 1877 off the coast of the small town of Ilo in Chile, 4500 miles south of San Francisco. 'HUASCAR' had turned pirate, having been seized by some failed revolutionaries who were interfering with British shipping besides trying to levy contributions ashore for their cause.

The flagship of the Royal Navy squadron at the time was H.M.S. SHAH, a steam, screw, sailing frigate of 6250 tons, under the command of Rear Admiral de Horsey. She was armed with two 9 inch guns, sixteen 7 inch, and eight 6.3 inch muzzle loaders, having been built at Portsmouth in 1873. 'SHAH' and 'AMETHYST' were the first two wooden ships to engage an armoured vessel.

The encounter took place at a range of 1900 yards and 'HUASCAR' was hit 65 times resulting in one killed and three wounded; the first Whitehead torpedo was fired in anger but failed to register a hit. The rebel ship managed to escape in the dark and the undamaged British ships claimed that this was due to the fact that the coastal town of Ilo was in their line of fire; nevertheless the clash appears to have achieved a satisfactory result. By way of interest it is reported that 'HUASCAR' survives to this day in a port on the coast of Chile.

Fifty years earlier, following the Battle of Waterloo, Britain, by way of her brilliant Admiral Cochrane (later Lord Dundonald), played a large part in the fragmentation of the Spanish/Portuguese Empire by destroying their fleets off South America and this ultimately led to the creation of independent states there.

As First Lieutenant and Gunnery Officer of 'AMETHYST', Bickford's skills were well tested by this action with 'HUASCAR' and consequently it enhanced his prospects considerably. The following year he was given leave on full pay as documented on his Certificate from the Commander of H.M.S. ROYAL ADELAIDE, his next ship.

This was something of a bonus as the matter of half pay which usually applied was a constant source of dissatisfaction among officers. After a ship had 'Paid Off' having completed a commission, her officers went on leave, on full pay. This only lasted for a short time, then they went on half pay which represented about a third of full pay. Consequently there was a great demand for ships for officers to go to sea as otherwise they and their families had to live in very difficult financial circumstances. There were times when several hundred Lieutenants were living on half pay and even Commanders could spend as much as two and a half years unemployed.

During such a state, junior officers were encouraged to attend a Naval College, such as the one at Portsmouth, where they could do courses in such subjects as Steam, Navigation and French etc. for which the successful obtained extra pay for additional qualifications. Moreover one of the attractions was that accommodation was provided at a low rental. However the College was a dreary place and many officers congregated at 'The Keppels Head', a public house on The Hard at Portsmouth, which they used as an unofficial Club; it was known as 'The Nut' because of its smoky atmosphere and brown stained walls; it is still used as a meeting place by naval officers.

By December 1878 Bickford had managed to secure his promotion and in the Autumn of the following year he was appointed Commander of the battleship H.M.S. THUNDERER stationed in the Mediterranean.

She spent a good deal of her time in the region of Malta and could often be seen at anchor in the Grand Harbour at Valetta. The ship was outstanding in terms of smartness and this reflected well on the efficiency of her Commander who was responsible for her general condition.

As a result of this, The Hon Sir Edmund Fremantle, Captain of H.M.S. INVINCIBLE, another battleship in the squadron at Malta, approached Commander Bickford privately to enquire whether he would be prepared to transfer to 'INVINCIBLE' as her present Commander was unsatisfactory and Fremantle wanted him replaced.

Bickford was placed in an awkward position, in spite of the compliment, which is revealed in personal correspondence. However, fortunately, the Commander-in-Chief, Admiral Sir Geoffrey Hornby, was not in favour of such a change and so the difficulty was resolved. Nevertheless it does show that the reputation of a good officer can extend beyond the realms of his own Wardroom.

After two busy years in 'THUNDERER' the Egyptian Campaign of 1882 began. The Turkish and native governments of the country disintegrated in an area of British commercial enterprise. In order to assist these interests, the European Powers gave naval and military support, under the guise of giving protection to the Suez Canal area and the native population from the misrule of Khedive Ismail; he was a spendthrift and through international borrowings he had nearly bankrupted Egypt.

Ismail offered his personal share holding in the Suez Canal Company for sale and it was promptly snapped up by Benjamin Disraeli. The Sultan of Turkey, responsible for governing Egypt, then deposed Ismail and appointed his son Tewfik who was prepared to accept foreign guidance, principally from the Anglo/French lobby in respect of Government finance. This led to an outcry with shouts of 'Egypt for the Egyptians' and an Egyptian Army Officer, Ahmed Arabi, supported by Ismail, appointed himself leader of the opposition to the rule of Tewfik, whose downfall they eventually secured.

Amid all this manoeuvring for position in the Government the fear for the safety of foreign nationals intensified and tension rose. Accordingly a force of French and British troops was sent to Egypt supported by a number of warships, to defeat Arabi. The French withdrew from the operation having more important duties in Europe, even though they had been very much involved in the area with the construction of the Suez Canal.

This meant that the British ships were left to support the land forces under the command of Wolseley, who was later made a Viscount, by undertaking a bombardment at Alexandria. It lasted nine hours and silenced Arabi Pasha's strongly fortified positions and led to the eventual British occupation of Egypt.

It was during the outbreak of these hostilities that Commander Bickford was transferred to the war zone where he was employed from 24th July to 20th October as Senior Commander of H.M.S. THALIA. She was engaged in transport duties covering the movement by sea of troops, horses, and stores besides such items as railway wagons, sleepers and other equipment for the construction of an armoured train used in the campaign.

Although the war was short, lasting from 20th August to 14th September 1882, it involved a great deal of heavy fighting. British casualties amounted to 52 killed, 30 missing and 382 wounded against over 3000 dead on the Egyptian side, who lost sixty guns from an army half as large again as the

British one; the successful outcome was all due to superior strategy and better equipment.

For his work as Senior Transport Officer in the war zone the Director of Transport at the Admiralty wrote to express his considerable satisfaction at the way in which the work had been carried out by Commander Bickford.

In addition he was awarded by the Egyptian Authorities decorations taking the form of the Khedive's Bronze Star and the Medjidie 3rd Class, for the tasks he had undertaken. The Sultan of Turkey, as has been said previously, was the established overall ruler of Egypt at the time; it was a Province of the Ottoman Empire, eventually becoming a British Protectorate and later an independent state.

Accordingly the Citation to the Award, headed with Sultan's monogram in stylised calligraphic format used on all ceremonial documents, when translated from old Turkish, reads: -

"This, the Sultan's noble and lofty document has been prepared in accordance with my illustrious Imperial decree issued on receipt of information from the Khedive of Egypt attesting the great merits of the British Naval Commander Andrew K Bickford, to award him the noble Order of the Medjidie, third Class.

26th February 1883 at Constantinoble."

CHAPTER II

THE NISERO AFFAIR

It was late in 1882 that Commander Bickford was at last given his first full command.

She was H.M.S. PEGASUS, a Composite Screw Sloop of 1139 tons measuring 170 feet, powered by steam and sail. She was built at Devonport and launched in June 1878; although not a large vessel she had a compliment of 140/150 Officers and men. Her armament was two 7 inch and four 64 pounder guns which gave her quite considerable fire power for her size.

At the time she was stationed in the Far East with frequent calls at Singapore and Penang where Commander Bickford took over as her Captain.

The Flag Officer of the China Station at the time was Vice Admiral Sir William Dowell, serving in Hong Kong. He was responsible for all ships operating on the Station and gave them appropriate instructions. These were mainly concerned with cruises and patrols in the area, partly as flag showing exercises and partly for the policing of the seas which were seldom free from disturbance.

to those on international business. Spices and commodities together with supplies from Europe and the Far East were carried and required protection from pirates, wreckers and local unrest; it was an important job which often went unrecognised.

Considerable distances had to be covered when carrying out this work remembering that in those days the Queen's Empire was enormous and spread over vast areas of the globe; the pink areas marked on Victorian maps indicate its great size. The shaded sections of Appendix III demonstrate this fact.

Having been recommissioned on 24th February 1883, the first substantive cruise of 'PEGASUS' from Penang began in the Autumn of that year. It was scheduled to cover an area which included the coast of the Malay Peninsular and the Straits Settlements which were separated from the Island of Sumatra (Indonesia) by the Malacca Straits.

The ship's instructions were to proceed to Oleh-Ch and Bûbûn on the coast where she was to remain for a period before sailing for Singapore after coast hopping.

Meanwhile on 8th November 1883 on the coast Sumatra, at a place called Bonga near Bûbûn, a British cargo ship s.s. NISERO of 1818 tons with a crew of twenty five, was wrecked. She was carrying a maximum cargo of 1200 tons of sugar requiring a reduced supply of coal which it was thought could be made up by calling at additional ports on the voyage if there should be any shortfall.

The calculations of coal usage were evidently wrong because after nine days supplies began to run low so the Captain had to alter course and make for the nearest port but unfortunately at 8.30 in the evening in stormy darkness the ship struck a reef. The engines went astern but to no avail and in order to avoid an explosion the gallant engineer opened the safety valves and there was a noisy escape of steam.

Fortunately the starboard lifeboats were undamaged so the crew scrambled into them and managed to struggle through the surf to the shore. It was very frightening for the men as they did not know where they were and there were dangers from sharks, wild animals and fierce local inhabitants.

Sadly five of the crew perished while the remainder, once ashore, were promptly taken prisoner by an armed local Chief acting for the Rajah of Tenom, a powerful Provincial Ruler who controlled four districts of the Province of Acheen. After such a harrowing ordeal this event did not constitute much of a reception for the wretched shipwrecked sailors.

News of the wreck became known by the Dutch two days after the disaster but London only heard about it two weeks later, on 23rd November, because of slow communications. In the meantime the local natives had stripped the ship of anything of value.

At the time of the incident the Rajahs were in dispute over their rights with the Dutch Colonists who has established themselves largely by force. Although a Treaty between Britain and Holland, in respect of Sumatra, had been established in earlier years it mainly covered the parties in regard to their respective colonial positions and the matter of Free Trade in the region. Accordingly the Dutch assumed the power of controlling trade and they treated the Rajahs as their subjects.

In these circumstances it is understandable that the Rajahs should think that by taking hostages it would help them to achieve their ends at a time of unrest.

The Dutch mounted a blockade of Acheen ports, which were very important to the local economy, on the pretext of a dispute over an unpaid pepper debt. It should be explained that the Rajah received pepper from producers as of right and then sold it through Acheen, the main trading centre of the area, and the Dutch were often the purchasers; in this case it seems that the payment was not forthcoming which inflamed the general situation still further.

The twenty survivors of 'NISERO' on arrival ashore were led to a detention centre situated on a sandy island area, a few yards off shore. Meantime the five sailors who had died were buried in a small cemetery which was fenced

H.M.S. Pegasus in harbour, 1880

off and marked with a single large cross and small crosses to mark each grave; two further graves were added later.

The captives on this island camp were provided with sleeping quarters in palm leaf roofed huts containing frame bunks and the compound was guarded by armed men. They were held in fear of their lives and had to undertake minor agricultural work and some fishing in order to survive for several months under very severe hardship. There was sickness with dysentery and cholera of which two subsequently died and the others became very weak.

The owners of the s.s. NISERO, D.G. Pinkney & Sons of Sunderland, attempted to persuade the Government to pay the wives of the crew half the pay of their husbands while they were captive, to alleviate hardship. Most of the sailors wives at home were without money and some almost destitute; the situation was such that months later the crew saw the Government as abandoning them in a remote, jungle land.

While the Acheenese had conciliatory relations with the British, whose protection they really wanted, they disliked the Dutch as colonisers intensely. Accordingly they were determined to use the captives as a lever to obtain some improvement in their political situation.

While this was going on, H.M.S. PEGASUS was still in Penang. She was instructed by the Commander-in-Chief to proceed to Acheen, the main port near Bonga, and deal with the affair as best her Captain thought fit, in consultation with the Governor of The Straits Settlements, Sir Fred Weld.

On Tuesday 19th February 1884 the Log of 'PEGASUS' records that at 4 o'clock in the morning the wreck of 'NISERO' was observed on the port beam and a Dutch gunboat 'BEUCOULIU' was at anchor, whereupon 'PEGASUS' stopped and communicated with her.

The temperature that morning was 65 degrees and 'PEGASUS' had been making way at three knots in light airs.

In the first instance there was great difficulty in obtaining permission from the Dutch to visit the wreck by anyone from 'PEGASUS' and then only by the persistence of her Captain. Initially he wanted to establish contact with the captives so as to arrange a method of regular communication with them by letter.

Eventually, messages began to pass and the British managed to get medicine, food and clothing to the crew.

Then the Dutch threatened the Rajah with punishment if the prisoners were not released but to no avail. Meanwhile further strenuous efforts were made by the British to converse with the local armed Chief to secure freedom for the prisoners. In this regard 'PEGASUS' returned to the scene of the wreck no less than four times but without success.

It should be mentioned that at the beginning of the previous December the Captain of the 'NISERO', with the aid of a Chinese to act as interpreter, had been sent by the Rajah of Tenom and his tutor, Tuku Yit, to Acheen to open negotiations with the Dutch. However, this was pre-empted by the Dutch Consul who, having been alerted to the situation, foolishly moved in on the Chief's village and burnt down eight huts as a reprisal; it is said that the captives would have been released but for this Dutch intervention.

When the Dutch realised that the British Navy was taking a serious interest in matters, they wanted an excuse to break off negotiations and so ignored the pleas that were being made. They sent the delegation on to another more important Rajah, the Sultan of Acheen, who they also disregarded because they did not want anyone else to rescue the crew if they were unable to do so themselves - it seems that national pride was at stake; at least this was the suggestion of the Captain of NISERO, who had not helped matters himself by breaking his parole and not returning to his crew for nineteen days. Additionally his conduct in dealing with the Dutch Consul was such that he seems to have destroyed the Rajah's confidence in European ways and substantially injured their reputation for honesty and fair play.

In the initial stages of negotiations this certainly frustrated the efforts of the Captain of 'PEGASUS' to persuade the Chief to accede to his demand to come under the control of a British warship either on board or on the beach.

BONGA, ON THE COAST OF SUMATRA, WHERE THE NISERO WAS WRECKED, NOV. 8, 1883.

SANDY ISLAND, WHERE THE CREW LIVED IN DETENTION.

CEMETERY OF THE SEVEN WHO DIED.

SHED INHABITED BY THE CAPTIVES.

WRECK OF THE NISERO, AS SEEN TEN MONTHS AFTER SHE GOT ASHORE.

NATIVE CANOE, STICK, AND PADDLE.

INSTRUMENT FOR CRUSHING PADDY.

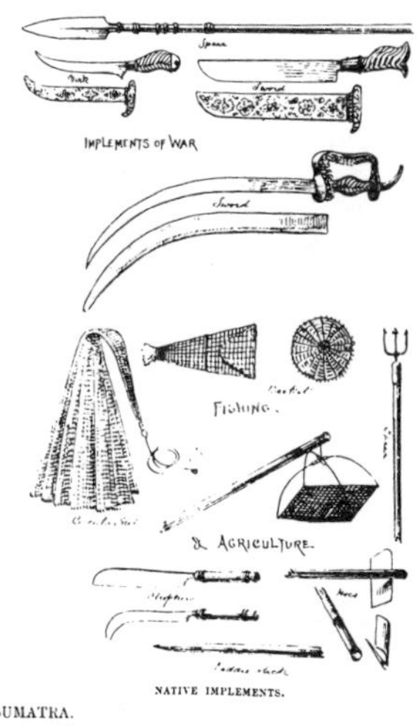

NATIVE IMPLEMENTS.

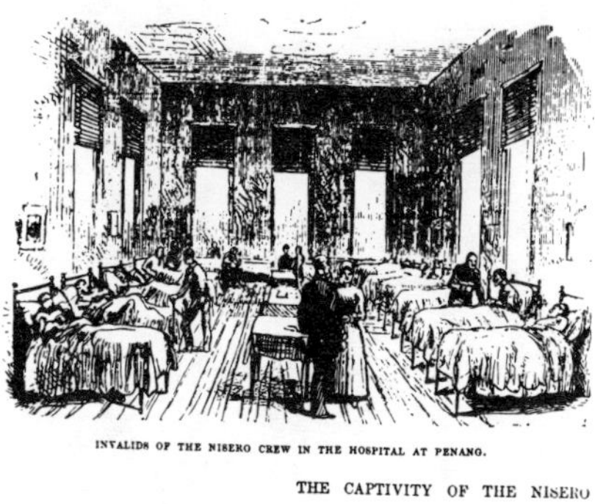

INVALIDS OF THE NISERO CREW IN THE HOSPITAL AT PENANG.

THE CAPTIVITY OF THE NISERO CREW IN SUMATRA.

(With permission of the Illustrated London News)

The Dutch and British Authorities, though not on the best of terms, co-operated to some extent and considered joint action if diplomacy failed.

It is worth recording that the Admiralty in London was not particularly interested in the matter as they considered it was a Foreign Office responsibility. Accordingly they decided to leave action in the hands of the officer on the spot, under the general direction of the Governor of the Straits Settlements. Matters did, however, become of international significance and were debated in the Dutch Parliament the following July.

An account of that debate in the Hague in 1884 reveals the strength of Dutch feeling towards Britain's intervention in the affair.

It was, of course, a complicated matter as the protection of the crew was paramount and at the same time the relative positions of Britain and Holland were involved in regard to the Straits Settlements and the Dutch East Indies. Last but not least there was the matter of the attitude of the Rajahs towards the Dutch which was causing concern as unrest among the population became an issue.

This latter situation was aggravated by the pepper debt and the sanctions which were being applied. The Rajahs were considered rebel pirates by the Dutch while the British association with Holland was suggested to be on the pretext of preventing the wrecking of British trading ships and the pirating of them.

The Dutch maintained that it was they who were the contributors to peace in this regard but got the poor end of the bargain. Moreover, it was pointed out that the blockade would probably end up being ineffectual as too many ships were required and the geography allowed it to be easily broken; additionally there was hardship for the crews and problems of maintenance of the vessels. All these matters made for a heated exchange of views in the Parliament in The Hague.

Reverting to the earlier situation, the Governor of the Straits Settlements had given full support to Commander Bickford's actions after obtaining permission to especially retain him for the operation; this is revealed in personal papers.

Sir Fred Weld, the Governor, was worried that in spite of his good relations with the Rajahs, if matters were left to the Dutch the captives would be killed.

As has already been said the Dutch were somewhat 'Dog in the Manger' about the whole affair and tried to frustrate the efforts being made to negotiate for the captives safe release by suggesting that presents offered at meetings as a normal courtesy by the Rajahs, should be refused - if this were done it certainly would have represented a snub and all communication would have been cut off and the prisoners slaughtered.

All manner of ideas were mooted by the British and Dutch Authorities to secure the release of the crew including the use of an overland force under European guidance. This was strongly opposed by Sir Fred as from his previous experience it would have necessitated the use of a substantial force of armed men, including some Dutch, and accordingly would have been disastrous. The Governor insisted on continued negotiation as he did not want Dutch involvement of any kind.

Accordingly in early January 1884, with the approval of Sir Fred Weld, Commander Bickford, accompanied by an officer on the Governor's Staff, decided to approach the local armed Chief at his Headquarters.

'PEGASUS' tried to reach the H.Q., which was up a river estuary, but the water was too shallow and it proved impossible. It was during this attempt that unfortunately, in an effort to sound the depth of the sand-bar, a whaler from 'PEGASUS' capsized and Leading Seaman Thomas and Able Seaman Curry were drowned.

In consequence 'PEGASUS' had to return to Penang where she collected stores and took on coal pending a return to Tenom to resume negotiations. In the meantime the Dutch were sending a punitive force of twelve hundred men to the Rajah. This was not helpful in respect of the efforts being made to release the crew which, in consequence, were not immediately successful.

During the ensuing months there were continual trips by 'PEGASUS' to Penang and Singapore to take on coal and stores for the trips to Acheen. On

PENANG, IN THE STRAITS OF MALACCA.

CHIEF OF BONGA.

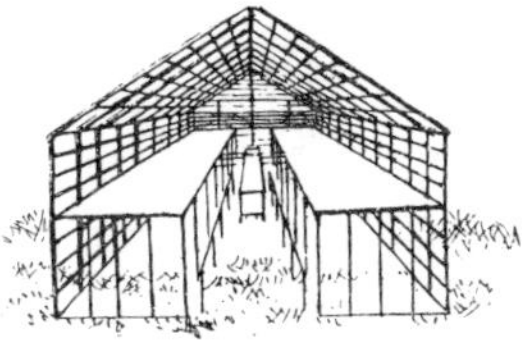

INTERIOR OF HUT, WITH FRAMES OF SLEEPING BUNKS.

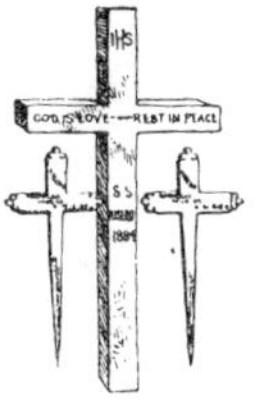

MONUMENTS OF THOSE WHO DIED.

THE GENERAL HOSPITAL AT PENANG.

H.M.S. PEGASUS, WHICH BROUGHT THE CREW OF THE NISERO TO PENANG.

BATAS, NATIVES OF THE INTERIOR.

1. James Grant, donkey-man. 2. Martin Michelson, seaman. 3. Laurence Muller, boatswain. 4. Ah Foo, second Chinese cook. 5. Franz Jacobson, seaman. 6. James Wilson, chief engineer. 7. Charles S. Crichton, chief officer. 8. J. Thompson, purchaser. 9. W. Bradley, third engineer. 10. Thomas Budd, third officer. 11. L. K. Moore, second officer. 12. John Stanton, fireman. 13. Carl Gronn, seaman. 14. Hanetar Haar, seaman. 15. George Essery, first steward. 16. John Kelly, fireman. 17. Olens Holgerson, seaman.

The photograph of an Italian, named Guatino Tasserio (seaman), could not be taken, owing to his illness.

THE SURVIVING CREW OF THE NISERO.

THE CAPTIVITY OF THE NISERO CREW IN SUMATRA.

(With permission of the Illustrated London News)

such journeys there was a routine of exercises and training drills in the ship to keep her in an efficient and smart condition and thus relieve any monotony that there may have been among the ships company.

However, there were some diversions, for instance while in Singapore on 8th June the Italian ship 'PROSPERITA' caught fire and immediately a call was made to 'PEGASUS' for help to extinguish the blaze. It was quite a hazardous operation but fortunately successful and Commander Bickford received a letter of thanks from the Italian Government which was passed to him via the Commander-in-Chief in H.M.S. VIGILANT at Hong Kong.

Commander Bickford, on a further visit to Acheen took with him two officers from the Colonial Service after deciding to make another personal approach, this time to the Rajah of Tenom. It was not without risk to himself and his party.

After a few weeks his intervention paid off partly due to diplomacy and correctness, and partly to his courage in visiting the Rajah on a mainly personal basis though, of course, he had the back-up of a warship at his disposal should things go wrong.

There were tedious days of argument but eventually the Rajah was told that if he released the men the blockade of his ports which was taking place would be lifted and trade resumed; this was a matter of great importance to him. Additionally a sum of 10,000 Dutch dollars would be paid to him on release of the men to extinguish the pepper debt and to pay for expenses in respect of the captives; it was emphasised that there was no real advantage in his continuing to hold the prisoners who, after all, had become uninvited guests in his country through no fault of their own.

However, he was told in no uncertain terms that if these conditions were not accepted, the Dutch and British forces would combine immediately and punish him and his people.

A deal was struck but there continued to be a good deal of bickering in regard to the payment of the money, owing to a measure of distrust on the part of the Rajah and the unhappiness of the Dutch over paying what they considered to be a ransom.

Initially the sum of 2000 Dollars was handled over for the release of an Italian seaman named Guitano Tasserio, who was in poor health, suffering from bronchitis. This was followed by further negotiations in respect of the amount and method of payment of the balance. Eventually this problem was resolved and according to custom, on 9th September 1884 under a large escort, the remaining crew of 'NISERO' were marched to a small trading village, handed over and taken on board 'PEGASUS'.

So it was that by early Autumn the evacuation of the crew had taken place and 'PEGASUS' was on her way back to Penang from Acheen. After a check up in hospital the survivors travelled directly back to London on board s.s. AJAX which sailed on 21st September 1884.

It had taken the best part of a year of patient negotiation, co-ordinated planning and hard work to secure a satisfactory outcome to this incident which was achieved without bloodshed and the maintenance of reasonable diplomatic relations with the Dutch.

Another task had thus been successfully carried out by the Royal Navy.

All these matters are recorded in private correspondence with the Governor of the Straits Settlements, Reports to the Admiralty and in the Press.

The very satisfactory conclusion, resulting from Commander Bickford's cool diplomacy, became the subject of a substantial number of letters of appreciation from the Governor of The Straits Settlements, The Foreign Office in the name of Earl Granville, The Admiralty and last but not least The Italian Government because of the early release of Guitano Tasserio, the very sick Italian seaman.

During subsequent months 'PEGASUS' carried on with her cruise to Lubuan, Brunei and the North Borneo Ports where she showed the flag as a sign of British sea power emphasising the security it could provide.

In February 1885 Commander Bickford, having received promotion to

Captain on 31st December, arrived back in England on leave, where a further letter of thanks was awaiting him; this time it was from The Secretary of State for Foreign Affairs passed on by the Admiralty.

With all the fuss and the outburst of congratulations no one was unduly surprised to hear of a nomination, by the Foreign Office, for an Award making Captain Bickford a Companion of the Order of Saint Michael and Saint George (C.M.G.); it was bestowed on him on 24th April 1885. Quite an achievement for a junior Captain with his first command at a comparatively young age.

For some time, following the receipt of this decoration, Captain Bickford enjoyed foreign service leave and he applied for an extension so that he could spend further time with his family prior to the birth of another child. In this respect he hoped that his next command might keep him nearer to home.

Eventually an Appointment arrived; it was not to a fighting ship as he had expected, but H.M.S. ASSISTANCE, a lightly armed Troop/Store ship of 2515 tons which he joined in 1887 as her Captain. Although it seemed to him to be an infill job, the opportunity of going to sea in this kind of vessel, though not really of his choice, was not to be spurned as her work was in support of the Home Fleet.

H.M.S. ASSISTANCE was engaged in general transport duties. She was making dozens of ferry trips to ports around the British Isles including some to Ireland and to the Channel Islands. Most of these sailings involved the delivery of service personnel, horses and stores etc.

Captain Bickford was the natural choice for this work following his successful time with transport during the Egyptian Campaign in earlier days. However, according to his Service Record, two years after joining the ship and scores of trips later, he unfortunately ran ASSISTANCE aground for twenty minutes off Harwich. Bickford was exonerated from blame and it was put down as a minor error, probably due to an inaccurate chart.

On 21st June 1890 he left the ship and moved on to commission H.M.S. MEDUSA for trials off Portland in July of that year. She was a 3rd Class

Cruiser of 2800 tons with an armament of six 6 inch guns and nine 6 pounders. Ships in this class were poorly designed and never achieved intended speeds. They were poor steamers having small boiler rooms leading to inefficient stoking; in addition the accommodation was cramped which made them altogether unsatisfactory as fighting ships. Not surprisingly the trials do not appear to have been entirely satisfactory as she was returned to Dockyard hands shortly afterwards and was paid off on 21st August. This meant that Captain Bickford had to content himself with a further period ashore, though from a personal domestic point of view it was probably quite welcome.

CHAPTER III

SAMOAN TROUBLES

Fortunately, from a Service angle, this period of unemployment did not last too long and Captain Bickford was appointed to H.M.S. KATOOMBA in March 1891 when she was first commissioned.

The ship was a smart Cruiser of the Pearl Class built by Armstrongs on the Tyne. While only small by many standards, being 2570 tons and 278 feet long, she was well armed and packed quite a punch with eight 4.7 inch Quick Firing guns and eight 3 pounder Quick Firing guns, supported by four machine guns and two 14 inch Torpedo Tubes.

She was paid for by Australia, as were others in the class, on the understanding that they would be stationed in Australian Waters but manned by the Royal Navy under Admiralty control.

Such ships were considered ideal for patrol work in the Far East and Pacific. Accordingly she took up position under the instructions of the Commander-in-Chief of the Australian Station, Rear Admiral Bowden Smith, early in 1892.

Initially her work was similar to that of 'PEGASUS' but this time it meant keeping an eye on the hundreds of islands and coral atolls representing outposts of Queen Victoria's Empire which were dotted all over the Pacific Ocean.

A good deal of business, in copra, fruit and spices etc. took place on an inter-island basis and also with Australia and New Zealand, to which trade the Navy afforded protection with its ships; they also provided support for the Authorities in respect of any unrest between traders and the various native populations.

Accordingly warships of the Royal Navy became quite a normal sight as they went about their business in island waters.

It may be helpful at this point to provide some background to the somewhat complicated state of affairs prevailing in Samoa at the time; more particularly, as Robert Louis Stevenson had a significant part to play at the time that 'KATOOMBA's' Captain was obliged to intervene in local political affairs at a time when the island Kingdom was supervised under an external tripartite arrangement.

Samoa consists of a single collection of islands in the Central Pacific among hundreds of other small islands, atolls and coral reefs stretching over a thousand miles or more; Western Samoa today makes up about two thirds of the whole of this group.

New Zealand is over two hundred miles to the South West and the coast of Australia lies at least three hundred and fifty miles to the West.

The Constitution and Sovereignty of Samoa in the late 19th Century was of an unusually complicated social order. It comprised an interwoven hierarchy of Kings and Chiefs where a feudal system prevailed and where there was constant discord leading to skirmishes and local wars; all this was increasingly influenced by the introduction of religious and missionary pressures.

The people themselves are of a delightfully happy, kind and generous disposition especially towards visitors to their islands. The men are tall and have a strong physique, while the women are appealing and good natured.

H.M.S. Katoomba c. 1890

(By permission of the National Maritime Museum, London)

All are musical and enjoy singing as is the case with so many Polynesian islanders.

Much of the background to the predominant situation in Samoa at the time under review is recorded in Robert Louis Stevenson's book "A Footnote to History" written in 1892.

Having spent a number of years of his life among the islands because of the climate which relieved his ill health, it also provided tranquillity for his writings to the extent that he finally built himself a house, 'Vailima', in Samoa where he lived and died at the age of 44; he was buried on an adjoining hilltop in 1894.

Stevenson's writings on these matters clearly indicate the prevailing atmosphere at the time. However, because of his particular style of composition, he is not always easy to follow, owing to the many and complicated issues that were involved.

Reports of Captain Cook's voyages of discovery in his ships 'RESOLUTION' and 'ADVENTURE' between 1768 and 1779 gave prominence to this region of the Central Pacific which previously was either unknown or had received relatively little attention. This resulted in a subsequent invasion of European adventurers who swarmed all over the islands and atolls.

The main port and trading mart of Samoa is Apia which was at the time a troublesome place with a rough, tough downtown area. It stands at the foot of a wooded mountain on a half moon shaped coast, having a barrier reef off-shore forming a lagoon in between, with a freshwater river running into it, providing a fine anchorage for many ships; palm trees abound and there is an area of mangrove swamp.

Early settlers consisted mainly of Germans who were engaged in building up an Empire under the Kaiser.

Recognising its attractions, an Agency was established in Apia in 1857 by the Hamburg firm of J.C. Godeffroy & Son. The Company then acquired large plantations under its Director Theodor Weber making it the most powerful commercial interest of any other Great Power. However the parent company in Germany went bankrupt as a result of speculative ventures such as trading in Russian paper and dealing in Westphalian iron.

The reconstituted successor to the original Samoan undertaking then acquired a lengthy German title which was abbreviated to 'D.H and P.G. of Hamburg' or just 'The German Firm'.

In this instance the business mainly consisted of producing and trading in copra, the growing of coffee and fruit, including pineapples for the Australian market, and the development of herds of cattle. The operations of the company were considerable to the extent that they led to the German Government taking a major interest in Samoan affairs.

It is said, however, that some £150,000 of English capital was invested in the company and that Barings of London, the Merchant Bankers, were involved in its formation.

The firm's estates, located behind the town of Apia, were well laid out in typical German fashion and consisted of about 10,000 acres with broad avenues enclosed by lime hedges and palm tree alleys. There were offices, stores and barracks for workers besides a fleet of company ships with Captains, Overseers, Cargo Superintendents and clerks; altogether a substantial and profitable undertaking.

The labour employed was partially local but 700/800 workers were imported under contracts of three to five years from such places as Fiji, New Caledonia, Hawaii and even Queensland, often having been recruited with false promises. Many of the managers were ex sea captains and there was maltreatment, while the business of labour imports was kept secret. As a result of punishment and abuse of workers there were many runaways and refugees from the estates roaming the islands.

In this venture the Germans were inspired by greatness of their country leading to patriotism in the extreme. This meant that small independent traders who were fighting for existence resented them and it lead to jealousy and disagreements. Meanwhile the German bosses lived the good life with walnuts and wine; they were lacking in humour, touchy and solemn.

Thus, a kind of German paternal colony, under the protection of the German Navy, was created within which the Samoan Kings and Chiefs played out their curious political lives with frequent disputes and wars.

Foreign influence had come about in 1887 when the Germans, who were supported by five warships lying off shore at Apia, deposed and deported the rightful monarch, King Malietoa Laupepa to the Marshall Islands, and replaced him with their own preferred candidate, another Samoan Chief named Tupua Tamasese. This resulted in strong opposition from the majority of the Samoan population who in consequence rallied round another Samoan Chief, Mataafa Iosefo.

In 1888 Tamasese improperly assumed the rightful King's title of 'Malietoa' whereupon Mataafa declared war upon him and proclaimed himself King also assuming the title of 'Malietoa'. During this time the Germans had almost total control over Samoan affairs and their Consul was in charge.

The other Powers, Britain and the United States, protested at Germany's general arrogant attitude towards matters and conflict between the three Great Powers was only averted by the hurricane of 1889 in which six of the seven ships in Apia harbour belonging to them, were destroyed.

Subsequently, in order to normalise relations between the controlling authorities, Germany convened a Conference on Samoan Affairs which was held in Berlin between April and June 1889. This agreed to release Laupepa from exile where he had been banished two years earlier.

This action was promoted, partly because of the German dislike of Mataffa whose forces had killed 18 Germans and wounded 36 others during a confused skirmish at Fangalie a year earlier. It happened when a German naval landing party had been despatched to protect some of the plantations from destruction, and to disarm rebels with whom they had been in conflict, over the German appointment of Tamasese as their puppet King.

Under the Treaty, the three Powers also agreed to recognise the independence of the Samoan Government and gave the free right of the natives to elect their Chief or King and to choose their form of Government. However, in view of the difficulties that surrounded elections in the confused state of the Government, the current holder of the office was to be recognised as King unless the three Powers, by common consent, should declare otherwise.

Accordingly it was decided that Malietoa Laupepa should again be accepted as King. This was a compromise to satisfy the German opposition to the appointment of Mataafa whose election they had prevented and to the American objection to Tamasese. The decision was finally confirmed by the three Governments and through their Consuls; after the Samoans had given way, a proclamation was issued in December 1889 rejecting the election of Mataafa and formally requiring Laupepa to be recognised as King.

Of the three Powers, supervising Samoan affairs, Germany was by far the most important with a strong trading presence by way of her long established plantation company. Britain and the United States were really junior partners in the arrangement although they had great influence.

The dominance of the Germans was displayed by frequently having two or more ships from the Kaiser's Navy at anchor while America and Britain usually had to rely on occasional visits by their ships to support their representatives. The harbour at Apia was of a size to take, in addition to warships, deep sea vessels, labour transports for 'The German Firm', as well as an island schooner.

The German Consul, though having a good deal of local power, often undertook to act on behalf of the German Government, because it took so long to secure their instructions; he sometimes went so far as to use their warships to support 'The German Firm' in its operations.

Not only did this create bad feeling among Samoans but there were also frequent quarrels over administrative matters with the other Powers which hardly made for stability. Apart from this situation there were in Samoa at that time both Catholic and Protestant Missionaries, in fact Apia boasted a

Roman Catholic Cathedral.

These religious communities supported the local people but it was often thought that they were involved in some of the intrigues which abounded. Sometimes it was felt that they represented an organ of civilisation pressing for reform and influence on local political affairs which, as religious, was not really their business.

Laupepa, having been reappointed King by the Three Powers, as a consequence of the Berlin Treaty, was often manipulated politically in Apia by the Germans; moreover he was not a Catholic which was to their advantage. On the other hand, Mataafa, who was still the desired choice of most Samoans, held a strong position being the hero of recent wars for which it was felt he should receive the fruits of victory.

In this respect, the Samoan people continued to insist that Mataafa should be their King because of their interpretation of the Berlin Treaty, but the Germans, as already stated, took up a strong stance against him having no confidence in or sympathy with his aspirations.

In 1891 Mataafa became frustrated and left Apia with some of his followers and proceeded to Malie, a native village seven miles south of Apia which had the right of conferring the Royal title of 'Malietoa'; his supporters wanted to declare him King there, as a symbolic gesture. In view of this he decided to live in the village where he styled himself 'King of Samoa' signing his correspondence as such and heading it 'The Government of Samoa'. He felt entitled to be considered a law abiding citizen and believed his attitude to be constitutional to the extent of sending offenders to the Chief Justice in Apia for trial and by paying taxes there.

It is, of course, true that Mataafa as a pretender was a sovereign Prince with authority and so he had some case for acceptance as King. He was tall and powerful and gave a sense of order and of economic ability, though sometimes he appeared to be somewhat rigid in accordance with his Catholic upbringing.

He probably would have made a much better ruler than Laupepa but the

Three Powers supported by their Consuls, having declared him a rebel, intended to take a firm line in this regard but they dithered. Among other suggestions it was proposed that he should have his estates confiscated but this would have aggravated an already inflamed situation.

For two years confrontational conditions between Laupepa's Government and Mataafa continued until in the Spring of 1893 when the frustrated and determined Mataafa hoisted his flag in defiance. Events were now leading to open conflict between the two antagonists and their supporters. Although the three Consuls had been trying to persuade their Governments to take firm action against Mataafa they continued to be indecisive. Eventually, Laupepa decided that he must act on his own so he began the slow process of assembling his Army, in spite of a lack of promises of support from the three Consuls who were still without instructions from their Governments.

In July the two warring sides faced each other near Apia with Mataafa defending his village position. In truth the initial confrontation was more like a village tea party than war with both armies fraternising and intermingling but, as if by accident, Laupepa attacked and it was not long before Mataafa's disorganised forces were forced to flee to the Island of Manono after destroying their village behind them. The King's forces too, were indecisive and disorganised and seemed more interested in discussion than following up their advantage; such were the ways of the Samoans.

Robert Louis Stevenson who was living in Samoa at the time was outraged when he realised the manoeuvrings and manipulation that was being carried on by all Three Powers who were ignoring the needs and traditions of the Samoan people.

Stevenson felt that Mataafa had been badly treated and would have made a better King; it seems that he had a personal regard and political respect for Mataafa and went so far as to try to secure reconciliation between the warring factions to avoid bloodshed.

In some quarters it was suggested that secretly Britain, through her Consul, recognised Mataafa's claim but he was disliked because he was a Catholic and they were reluctant to disturb a situation which suited them; in fact such stories were probably untrue and may have been given credence by the Protestant London Missionary Society which was provided with an opportunity to promote its own particular cause in the islands at a time when there were suggestions that the Catholic Missionaries were siding with Mataafa and his followers.

Stevenson expressed his feelings in regard to the general situation in his letter of Tuesday 18th July to his close friend Sidney Colvin and he opens by observing that on the previous Sunday, 'KATOOMBA', with Captain Bickford C.M.G in Command, had arrived.

He goes on to say that a day earlier (Monday) he had gone down with Graham (Graham Balfour, his cousin) to call, and found that Bickford had orders to suppress Mataafa at once, requiring him to go down, before daybreak, to Manono. Stevenson remarked that he thought Bickford to be a very capable and energetic man and wished he had come ten days earlier so that the current situation could have been avoided. However matters had subsequently developed to the extent that there were many awkward questions to be answered.

He posed these by asking firstly, would Mataafa surrender? Secondly, would the people consent to being disarmed and what would happen if they did? Finally, what would any of them believe after all the former pretence, particularly as the three Consuls were currently unavailable having gone off to see the King; in this respect Stevenson was particularly annoyed that Cusack-Smith, the British Consul, was not available to deliver a letter he had written, with some effort, to Mataafa.

Some modern authors seem to be of the view that Stevenson got on well with Bickford, whom he described in friendly terms, and it seems that a number of discussions took place between the two men. It is said that Stevenson had a particular affinity with the sea and mariners, probably due to the family's occupation of design and construction of lighthouses for which they are famous. Additionally Stevenson was a pragmatic man in some respects having had a grounding in the legal profession during his early years.

As it was 'KATOOMBA' had arrived in Auckland, New Zealand, prior to the deteriorating situation in Samoa, where she received orders from Rear Admiral Bowden Smith, Commander-in-Chief Australia Station.

She was told to proceed to Apia at moderate speed and to comply with Admiralty instructions. These stated that there was to be co-operation with the other two Powers there, so as to demonstrate to the rebels (Mataafa) the futility of resistance and to secure peace and stability of Government, if possible, without bloodshed. There were fears for the safety of the white population but only after the King had finally decided to pursue Mataafa and his followers who had fled to Manono, was a British warship really considered necessary.

The instructions went on to confirm that any proceedings in support of the Government were to be entirely at the discretion of the Naval Commanders of the Three Powers concerned, after consulting together and with their respective Consuls; attention to 'The Final Act of Conference on Samoa 14th June 1889' was to be observed. Up to this point the Three Powers had dithered over taking firm action and the Germans would not act until vessels from the other two Powers arrived.

Captain Bickford, the senior Naval Commander, was authorised to retain, if necessary, the services of two other ships, H.M.S. RINGDOVE and H.M.S. RAPID, the latter ship being in the Gilbert and Ellice Islands with the High Commissioner for the Western Pacific on board.

If one ship was to remain at Apia the Commander-in-Chief preferred 'RAPID' as 'KATOOMBA' needed to go into dock. However it was decided that she should stay with Bickford in overall charge as he was particularly conversant with the situation. In any event all ships were instructed to withdraw before the start of the hurricane season.

This latter order was very appropriate because, as reported by Stevenson in "A Footnote to History", four years previously in March 1889, a terrible hurricane struck Apia with mountainous seas and winds of terrific force. Of seven warships belonging to the Three Powers in the anchorage at the time, only one, H.M.S. CALLIOPE, commanded by a Captain Kane Royal Navy, survived; the remainder, their boiler fires having been extinguished, were wrecked and there was considerable loss of life.

On arrival, Captain Bickford, having conferred with the parties ashore as instructed, decided that there was no alternative but to issue Mataafa with an ultimatum. Accordingly, a document was drawn up on board 'KATOOMBA' in the name of the three Treaty Powers and the ships escorted the King's war boats to Manono where the paper was presented to Mataafa on board 'KATOOMBA'.

Briefly it stated that Mataafa and his Chiefs, eighteen in number, should come on board 'KATOOMBA' within three hours of receipt of the document. If he refused the three ships, 'KATOOMBA' and the German 'BUSSARD' and 'SPERBER' would open fire on him and the King's forces, would attack from the mainland.

All his arms were to be delivered to the ship and then, all but Mataafa with his Chiefs were to remain on board while the remainder of his party was required to return to the Island of Manono. If there was non compliance with this demand and fighting broke out, all the women and children were to be sent alongside the warship for protection thus ensuring that they would be safe.

Fortunately the official pressure that had been applied to Mataafa was sufficient and the following day a signed paper arrived from him with agreement to all the demands of the Three Powers. This was largely due to the intervention of Father Broyer of the Catholic Mission, with whom Captain Bickford, who was a Catholic himself, had a good rapport; the Priest had great influence with the natives and was anxious to avoid bloodshed.

Stevenson had earlier written a personal letter to Mataafa for delivery by Cusack-Smith, as already mentioned, imploring him as a friend to surrender to Captain Bickford; this communication was supposed to have been delivered at the time of the ultimatum but the Consuls objected and it was only handed to him after the surrender had taken place.

Initially, to back up the terms of the ultimatum, preparations for an assault had been made. These included the use of the warships of the three Powers which would escort 126 war boats of the King who would have 1500 of his warriors standing by on shore. Their use was not ultimately necessary and in accordance with the terms of the agreement some 90 stands of arms were brought on board 'KATOOMBA' in addition to 100 stands which were taken by the King on shore.

In so far as Stevenson was concerned with these matters some commentators suggested that he was merely an innocent onlooker whilst others treated him more harshly intimating that he was a meddling troublemaker, when really his main concern was the good of the Samoan people.

Captain Bickford's relationship with Stevenson, seems to have been socially cordial in as much as Fanny Stevenson, his American wife, described in her diary, one of several visits he made to their home.

In a letter from Stevenson to Sidney Colvin, a close friend, there is a graphic account of a visit by 'KATOOMBA's' band to Vailama where it had been asked to play in accordance with a request by Stevenson to Captain Bickford. This special event was obviously a great success as the letter records how the occasion formed one of the Stevensons brightest days.

There is a description of how fourteen smiling members of the band with instruments snaked their way up the mountain to the house followed by a group of happy children. The property seems to have been decorated with scented greenery for the occasion and the nine out-door workers, together with a working party which had been engaged out of kindness to pay their war-fines, were on hand to greet the party; a number of Samoan ladies were available to look after the children.

It seems that all manner of special food had been prepared including chicken, ham, cake and fruits which were served with coffee and lemonade, throughout the afternoon; for further refreshment, claret negus flavoured with rum and limes was handed round.

The band played and there was dancing, singing and acrobatics. The boys

Robert Louis Stevenson and his wife with the band of H.M.S. Katoomba, 1893
(With permission of Mrs Alanna Knight)

from the house then made an entry from the end of the veranda and performed a dance for the guests. It appears that such was their enthusiasm that it was difficult to get them to stop but in the event there was no trouble as the performance was adhering to a timetable.

At the end of the visit three cheers were given for the Stevensons and the band shook hands, formed up, and marched off playing. There seems to have been a sudden upset when a kicking horse in the paddock stopped the band from playing and someone thought the big drum had been ruined but Simele, one of the staff, dashed to the rescue and all seems to have been well. They carried on playing and wound their way down the hill with further bugle calls leaving their hosts happily exhausted. As the guests departed it was declared to have been one of the most successful occasions that had ever taken place.

A striking comment made by Stevenson in his letter was that the blue jackets had behaved particularly well and were considered to be such an interesting bunch of men; he felt that the navy was giving boys an education to make them special and suggested that they were a kind of low-class public school boy who was well mannered, fairly intelligent and sentimental, which was not unusual among sailors. Thus concluded Stevenson's description of the event.

Following the surrender of Mataafa the three Consuls who had been on board 'KATOOMBA' were then taken by one of the supporting German ships and put ashore in Apia. Expecting to return to Apia himself and much to Bickford's surprise and annoyance, it was found that the King's forces, who were supposed to return to their quarters, had attacked the Island of Manono and burnt down several houses. Consequently a message was sent, via the American Consul, to the King holding him responsible for any loss of life and for any further attacks that might be made on the now defenceless people of the island; in fact it seems likely that the raid that had taken place was not authorised by the King and action was taken against the perpetrators who were thought to consist of a group of 100 rogue supporters.

The following day 'KATOOMBA' did return to Apia with thirty-six prisoners remaining on board with a view to transferring them to various warships pending a decision of the Consuls and the King. It was noted that the officer in charge of the German ships had been particularly helpful to Captain Bickford in the course of these operations.

After the Consuls had met with the King and having discussed matters, they issued a signed directive, requiring that Mataafa and the Chiefs, on board the warships, be deported from Samoa as quickly as possible to some safe place.

It was felt that the longer the Chiefs remained on board the more plotting and intrigue there would be; it would take very little to stir up more trouble.

Moreover the Government strongly objected to allowing the Chiefs to take their women with them saying that it would be against Samoan custom. The atoll of Fakaofu to the North, which was a British Protectorate where Samoan was spoken, was suggested as a suitable place of temporary confinement as it had been used satisfactorily before in similar circumstances; accordingly the captives were taken there but they were subsequently moved to the Marshall Islands towards the end of the year.

The directive was to be kept secret as any farewell demonstration might get out of hand. A Government official was to accompany the prisoners to act as interpreter and make arrangements for their maintenance on behalf of the Samoan Government; he could then return in the warship.

Captain Bickford was not happy about this arrangement as is revealed in a private letter from the Governor of Fiji, who had been consulted as a personal friend. The letter indicated that the Governor was sending a telegram to Lord Ripon, the Colonial Secretary, suggesting that Mataafa should be taken to Fiji where he would be safe rather than the cruelty of sending him to the Marshall Islands. The support of Sir Robert Duff, the Governor General, in Sydney, was sought in the matter as it was confidently thought that he could apply some pressure on Downing Street.

The letter acknowledges that the German Naval men involved had also seen the injustice of sending Mataafa to "the wretched islands in the North". It goes on to comment that the Governor himself had studied both parties to the conflict and others in Samoa and he was very glad not to have had anything to do with them "since the Act of Berlin saw light". However, he said that he would do all possible to get his old friend out of the mess into which he had fallen or been led. The communication ends up by wishing Bickford a good voyage and finally by sending good wishes to the Commander-in-Chief and his wife.

'KATOOMBA' did not have sufficient coal for the voyage to the atoll of Fakaofu to deport Mataafa and his party, as delivery of it had not been received from Auckland. It was therefore decided that the German light cruiser 'SPERBER' should carry out the mission and so she left on 26th July with Mataafa and his principal Chiefs on board.

In spite of Mataafa's later banishment to the German controlled Marshall Islands to the north, Stevenson continued to support him by attending to some of his needs whilst in exile. Mataafa was confined to a life away from Samoa for five years until in 1898 he was released on condition that he signed a sworn affidavit pledging loyalty to the King but following the death of Laupepa he was elected King by his followers.

This caused to further conflict with the Powers who did not agree with this idea and it led to a bombardment of Mataafa's forces by United States and British ships. A settlement was eventually negotiated and the Kingship arrangement was abolished by the Powers who agreed to partition Samoa between Germany and the United States; in return Britain gave up her interests for German concessions elsewhere.

Germany ruled Western Samoa until 1914 honouring Mataafa (who died in 1912) as a Paramount Chief. New Zealand took over control after World War I and in 1962 Samoa became an independent state.

Reverting to the events of 1893, on 27th July coal for 'KATOOMBA' did arrive and was taken on board at Pango Pango where ships could lay alongside; it was difficult at Apia because of the swell. Whilst there, it was found that fighting had broken out among rival Chiefs nominally of the party of the King and Mataafa but really it was over jealousies of title.

The Chiefs, once they were told, on board 'KATOOMBA', by Captain Bickford, that the Civil War in Samoa was over through the action of the Three Powers, this local fighting died away.

On returning to Apia all was quiet and things had settled down amazingly well. Accordingly the British Consul did not consider it was necessary to retain a warship if a visit of such a vessel could be made occasionally but out of the hurricane season which was approaching.

The dangers of hurricanes are always considerable but especially in those days when vessels with masts and sails were less able to cope with such eventualities. In the previously reported storm of 1889 so many ships were wrecked that for a considerable time afterwards a collection of salvage was undertaken because both Islanders and Europeans were anxious to rescue anything of value for use ashore.

As to the account of developments, an official visit to the King on 9th August 1893 was arranged for the British Consul and three officers from 'KATOOMBA'. The King was congratulated on the termination of the rebellion due to the action of the Three Powers and he was advised that, together with his Chiefs and all the people of Samoa, the Powers were determined to uphold his authority and hopefully, as a result, his subjects would acquiesce and settle down quietly.

The King replied that he and his Chiefs realised the debt they owed to the Powers and they had not expected to receive the backing which had been given. However, they would have put down the rebellion in any event but they were particularly delighted that, with the help of the Powers, this had been achieved with such happy results; the action taken was compared to Moses stretching out his hands over the Red Sea for the Israelites to cross!

A Royal Kava or toast was then drunk in an elaborate ceremony. Captain Bickford responded by thanking the King for his friendly reception and by inviting him and his party on board 'KATOOMBA'. This was duly arranged and the ships company went to general quarters and worked the guns and torpedoes for their guests; the visit ended with a 21 gun salute for the King which was much appreciated.

In Captain Bickford's report to the Secretary of the Admiralty he pointed out that in all probability the troubles would never have occurred but for the European Powers who were represented by five highly paid officials with undefined powers; a case of 'too many cooks spoiling the broth'.

He stated that the natives were no fools and on seeing a lack of accord they were inclined to play off one party against another. The rebel party never believed that the Powers would unite against their leader, Mataafa, and act in favour of the King because of the indecision that was displayed. If there had been clearer direction the outcome would probably have been different.

Moreover, as has already been said, there was a certain section of troublemakers in the Samoan community who suggested that the Catholic Missions had encouraged Mataafa supporters in their actions against the Government.

This matter was carefully investigated, including consultation with those having both religious and secular views, and the assertions were found to be groundless; it was nothing but a troublesome invention. In fact the Missionaries tried to impress on Mataafa that, as the Powers had established the King's position, it was his duty not to oppose him. They would probably have succeeded but for the inaction of the Three Powers.

As for Mataafa, he had acquired an inflated view of his importance through all the attention he was receiving and he came to believe that he was the rightful King in spite of events.

However in all the circumstances it was deemed best for Mataafa and his Chiefs to stay out of the country for sometime. Captain Bickford, however, insisted that they should be allowed their wives in spite of the objections of his colleagues who maintained it was against Samoan custom. Bickford regarded it as an unnecessary piece of cruelty and a mistaken policy as the women would only plot in favour of their husbands and stir up further unrest. Moreover his compassion for the prisoners was amply demonstrated by the outspoken views he expressed.

Stevenson wrote a long letter to The Times dated 23rd April 1894 among many others, complaining about the deportation of Mataafa and of his being under German authority. Additionally he pointed out the injustice of fining Mataafa's supporters the enormous sum of £6600 for their activities which the Authorities had considered illegal.

He goes on to suggest that the King's troops did not behave in a disciplined manner, mentioning the prevalence of head hunting, which was not unknown, besides other uncontrolled activities, as instanced by their burning and pillaging on the Island of Manono.

The letter reports that on his knees Mataafa implored Captain Bickford to provide protection for women and children from the King's forces which, of course, had been done.

The tone of this correspondence is of general complaint about the Treaty of Berlin and of its effect on the Government of Samoa. Stevenson was in constant touch with events so he could write with considerable authority.

In a further letter to J.F. Hogan, a British Member of Parliament, dated 7th October 1894, Stevenson again complains about the action taken in deporting Mataafa to the Marshall Islands, in a German ship, instead of to Fiji. In this matter he tends to exonerate Captain Bickford from the course of action taken, realising that he was acting on instructions; the fact that 'KATOOMBA' was without sufficient coal to carry out the job of transporting Mataafa thus necessitating the use of a German vessel was obviously known to him as it is mentioned in Fanny Stevenson's diary.

After the turmoil of these events, by mid August 1893 conditions had quietened down sufficiently for the various warships to be dispersed.

Accordingly 'KATOOMBA' proceeded to Pango Pango to coal ship and on interviewing the previously warring Chiefs it was found that the antagonists wished to come to terms and submit to the decision of the Three Powers and to the Government.

After securing a guarantee of safety from the King in Samoa and a declaration of religious freedom because the people feared that they would be persecuted as Roman Catholics, the natives returned to their homes; this latter declaration was negotiated with the condition laid down by the Three Powers that the parties should be disarmed, but it was done without consulting the naval commanders.

It was pointed out by Captain Bickford, supported by the senior German naval officer, that such disarmament was out of the question without a properly disciplined native force of three or four hundred native men, which was not available, supported by warships. Such a force had to be strictly controlled otherwise there would be a repeat of the action by forces of the King who earlier had been involved in the destruction of houses and the crops of Mataafa's supporters on Manono Island, although he had already surrendered.

Moreover the ships would neither be able to control the action nor could the arms be captured for certain because they might be hidden. It would cause uproar in the whole country just when it was beginning to calm down with the acceptance of the King's authority.

In spite of these protestations the Consuls in Apia insisted that a party of government officials should visit Pango Pango and issue a Proclamation on behalf of the King and the Three Powers, under the guns of warships; the warring Chiefs were told that they must obey the King's commands and return to Apia to face trial for disobedience.

The operation was successful and substantial help was again given by the senior German naval commander, though Bickford's relations with the representatives of the Three Powers in Samoa do not appear to have been altogether so cordial on this occasion on account of their actions.

In fact it took a little while to secure full approval from the Foreign Office to Captain Bickford's operations in Samoa in respect of the deportation of Mataafa. However, on subsequent receipt of the full report of the Commander-in-Chief, Australia, not only was Bickford's action strongly endorsed, but letters of Commendation were forthcoming from the Foreign Secretary, the Earl of Rosebery, who appreciated that the major problems in Samoa had been solved for the Foreign Office/Colonial Office by the diplomacy and tasks undertaken by 'KATOOMBA's' Captain.

The ship, on orders from the Admiralty via the Commander-in-Chief, was now withdrawn from Samoan waters because of the approaching hurricane season. This was also desirable because there was a serious outbreak of measles in Apia and 'KATOOMBA' wished to avoid the infection of any of her ships company.

Accordingly she sailed from Samoa without delay. Having reached the port of Suva in Fiji, her captain called on his confidant the Governor, who had communicated with him and given advice during the Samoan troubles.

On 19th October, having taken on coal for her journey to Australia she left Suva for Norfolk Island and Lord Howe Island where she called briefly, communicated with the shore, and went on her way. During the voyage the rifles belonging to Mataafa's party were thrown overboard and on 27th October 1893 she passed Sydney Heads. KATOOMBA remained in Sydney for maintenance and repairs until 30th December when she finally left for Melbourne and Tasmania.

On 23rd February 1894, Captain Bickford left the ship for his return journey to England.

CHAPTER IV

THE CHANNEL SQUADRON

Following his arduous commission in the South Pacific there was a period of well earned leave which gave Bickford an opportunity to spend time with his wife and family in Southsea.

Then, on 1st February 1895, the appointment as Captain of the battleship H.M.S. RESOLUTION of the Channel Squadron under the command of Admiral Lord Walter Kerr, was received with much satisfaction.

In 1858 the Channel Squadron had been created to restore public confidence in the Navy at home, following the main and unending task, in which it had been engaged in earlier years, of protecting trade and keeping the peace throughout the far flung Empire.

A short time after the creation of this force, all the ships involved were ironclads. Their time was spent showing the flag around the British Isles besides making visits to ports in Scandinavia to the north and as far south as Gibraltar and the Canary Islands.

The intervening routine consisted of manoeuvres and war exercises which included the firing at targets on a competitive basis. At one time there were two Squadrons each having as many as five battleships and two cruisers competing against each other with some ships disguised as merchant vessels. It must have been quite a sight to see those great lumbering giants with a speed of only ten to fifteen knots manoeuvring tactically into position in the course of such operations.

It is known that in the course of one exercise 'RESOLUTION' fouled 'REPULSE' and this is noted on Bickford's Service Record. It remarks that it was due to poor ship handling and although an appropriate comment, the purpose of the exercise was partly designed to expose such shortcomings when a number of large and unwieldy vessels were operating at close quarters; on this occasion there were six battleships in the Squadron concerned.

In January 1896 Captain Bickford was appointed an aide-de-camp (A.D.C.) to Queen Victoria and this honour involved him in a number of official attendances over the next three years.

After serving in 'RESOLUTION' for about 18 months there followed an immediate appointment to H.M.S. INFLEXIBLE as Captain of the Fleet Reserve at Portsmouth which lasted a further two years.

The Fleet Reserve consisted of ships ready for sea at short notice and many were tied up in Portsmouth harbour. As Dockyards were more interested in building ships than repairing them some were neglected and not ready when required. The scheme was to take ready ships out of the hands of the Dockyard and make the Commander-in-Chief responsible for their efficiency when they were required.

Two Divisions, A and B were created. A Division, consisted of ships ready within 48 hours notice and B Division consisted of ships requiring slight repairs which could be made ready within fourteen days, while finally there was the Dockyard Reserve which comprised ships requiring extensive repairs.

The Commander-in-Chief could move ships from one Division to another and could influence the Admiral Superintendent of the Dockyard but he could not insist on repairs to defects. This position naturally led to conflict

The Captain of the "Resolution" and his A.D.C.
(Army and Navy Illustrated, 1896)

from time to time, naval officers always maintaining that ships were made for Dockyards not the other way round. In terms of the whole policy the Admiralty seemed to support the Dockyards as against the Fleet Reserve.

A further but lesser task which befell Fleet Reserve officers was the inspection of Coastguard establishments which controlled 'districts' covering long strips of the coastline of Britain.

The Captain of a Coastguard ship was in charge and there was an inspection once a year by a Fleet Reserve officer which also included the Royal Naval Reserve drill ships and batteries which were tested for efficiency; these were situated in the larger coastal centres. For example in Scotland, they were located in Dundee, Aberdeen, Inverness and other ports; manning was often by whalers and sealers who could attend parades in the winter evenings when they were at home. Chief officers were sometimes old Customs men and quite knowledgeable but the remainder of the crews were somewhat rough and ready.

In view of his background, with Fleet Reserve knowledge, it was logical that Captain Bickford should be appointed Captain of H.M.S. WILDFIRE in January 1898; she was the supply vessel to Sheerness Dockyard at the mouth of the Thames estuary.

The following year, in June 1899, he was made Captain Superintendent of the Dockyard and provided with his own residence. However it was said of Sheerness that it was "the last place God made" which gives some idea of the depressing nature of the area. Being a Dockyard it was like a gigantic scrapyard with boilers, pipes, propellers, anchors, and cables all lying about.

There is a story that on one occasion when a certain dignitary was visiting the Captain Superintendent, he noticed on arrival at the Dockyard that there were three scruffy urchins, two boys and a girl, playing about among the old boilers and scrap. Upon enquiring of the Policeman on the gate why they were allowed to be there, the reply came "I'm afraid, Sir, they're the Captain Superintendent's children so I can't stop 'em" - there was little more to be said!

CHAPTER V

COMMANDER - IN - CHIEF

On 15th October 1900 after fourteen months at Sheerness a personal letter arrived from the Admiralty offering Bickford, a newly promoted Rear Admiral, immediate Command of the Pacific Station at Esquimalt, British Columbia, as a result of the transfer of Rear Admiral Beaumont to the Australian Station.

This somewhat unexpected opportunity was grasped with both hands. The chance of a seagoing job after a period ashore at the somewhat depressing Dockyard at Sheerness raised his spirits considerably. Apart from anything else it was a great compliment to his ability and opened the door to even further promotion. Once again his reputation seems to have assisted with the offer of the appointment and possibly the friends he had made along the line had put in a good word for him.

Following this surprise he quickly made arrangements for the journey across Canada to pick up the flagship using the Canadian Pacific Railway in accordance with instructions which also suggested that before leaving he should consult with Prince Louis of Battenberg, a Director of Naval Intelligence at the Admiralty. This was presumably to give him an up to date briefing on the difficult political situation which existed between Great Britian and the United States in respect of a dispute over Canadian interests in northern Pacific waters, to which reference is made in the following pages.

Accordingly, at this point, it seems worth providing a brief historical background to the Pacific Station and the Esquimalt Naval Base in particular.

The Pacific Station came into being in 1837 when it was separated from the 'Brazils', often called the 'South American', station covering the South Atlantic which had Rio as its headquarters; it was initially created when the Portuguese Royal Family moved from Portugal to Bahia in Brazil having been escorted by six battleships, in 1808.

The original station was made up of Royal Navy ships supported by store-ships, and later with coaling facilities, which were positioned at various ports on the South American Pacific coast, controlled from Valparaiso in Chile and supported by Callao in Peru.

Meanwhile Fort Vancouver in British Columbia had been established on the Columbia River in 1830 to defend the fur traders of the Hudson Bay Company from Indians and other potential threats. This led to an increasing need for the support of Naval vessels more especially when the fur business grew into a seaborne operation superseding the overland route to London; in addition a general shipping trade was developing rapidly. Accordingly the Royal Navy required a suitable harbour for use by its ships.

Esquimalt, in a magnificent position, on the southern tip of Vancouver Island adjoining Victoria, the capital city of British Columbia, had provided an anchorage since 1837. Around 1846 three wooden huts were built as a temporary hospital for the sick and wounded from Royal Navy and survey ships; these buildings were used by the Royal Engineers who were surveying the Canadian/United States boundary line. When the Detachment left in 1852 the buildings with land were transferred to the Royal Navy in whose hands they remained until 1905 when the Naval base was run down and subsequently transferred to the Canadian Government.

In its earliest years, the establishment increased in size slowly and in 1857 when news of the formation of a shore base at Esquimalt on the Northwest coast became known to those serving on the South American coastal stations, there was great rejoicing as it meant that they were likely to be moved; conditions on these maritime outposts were not popular owing to the fact that they were uncomfortable, located in foreign waters, the language and money were difficult, and the climate was hot and dry.

The original hospital huts were supplemented after some time with an additional range of buildings to provide a depôt for provisions and stores etc. Then came the need for the ability to revent used naval guns, locally, which led to the creation of a complete dockyard with a graving dock and other repair facilities. To serve the needs for ammunition by the increasing number of Royal Navy ships using the facilities at Esquimalt, a magazine was built on Cole Island, at the head of the harbour, in 1860.

There was a long running dispute between the Governments of Britain and Canada over who should bear the cost of the base and of its defences, to the extent that other locations were given consideration but matters were finally resolved by compromise on the basis of half responsibility by each party.

One of the most contentious issues was the cost of the graving dock which was essential because the nearest repair facility requiring a dock was located in the United States at Mare Island, San Francisco and costs of work there were high and subsequently proved to be about double those at Esquimalt; alternative facilities were even further away which created an altogether unsatisfactory security situation.

Accordingly a dock, 400 feet long by 90 feet wide, and large enough to take ships of 7322 tons was constructed and opened in 1887 having taken three years to complete at substantial cost. Advocates for its establishment were vindicated in that twenty four merchant ships and seventy warships used it in the first seven years of its life.

The defences of Esquimalt were of constant concern particularly as relations between Britain and the United States were not the most cordial following an attempt to annex Canada prior to 1814; apart from anything else it was only about one hundred years since the American War of Independence had taken place.

Commander-in-Chief Pacific Station, 1901
Rear Admiral A.K. Bickford C.M.G. with his wife, daughter, Captain C Keppel RN, Flag Lieutenant and Secretary.

There was also a threat from Russia from across the Bering Sea. She had been at war with Turkey, a British ally, in 1877 so it was felt that her ships might be given an excuse to attack Victoria, shell the dockyard, and seize the substantial collieries situated on the east coast of Vancouver Island.

There were various reports from San Francisco of Russian warship movements and there was a suspicious, so called mistake, by a squadron of small Russian warships which entered Esquimalt harbour in 1885 possibly to survey its defences and altogether these events caused a war scare; so far as the intruders were concerned, the ships left after receiving orders but without providing any particular explanation.

It was because of this episode that two Torpedo Boats, numbers 39 (the SWIFT) and 40 (the SURE), were purchased from Chile to give some, if only small, additional strength to the Station. They sailed 6000 miles, escorted firstly by H.M.S. PELICAN and then by the steam corvette H.M.S. SATALITE, to Esquimalt which was quite a voyage as they were only 100 feet long and of 40 tons displacement. Initially they were provided with spar torpedo launching gear but later dropping equipment was fitted. They served on the Station until 1903 and then went into reserve being finally sold in 1905.

Their contribution to defence may not have been great but as a precaution against the threat of hit-and-run Russian cruisers and for training they served a useful purpose at a time when it was the guns of Royal Navy ships that constituted the harbour's main protection from attack.

Initially the shore defences were very poor and consisted of crude batteries of cannon taken from redundant ships and it was not until 1878 that the first real British and Canadian artillery protection was given by way of gun emplacements on Finlayson Point and Macaulay Point, with Brothers Island covering the approaches to the harbour entrance; later in 1900 fixed mine defences, which could be electrically detonated, were set up. A long running series of complaints to the Admiralty over the inadequacies of the defence of such an important Naval headquarters had taken place and Rear Admiral Bickford was not alone in the views he expressed on the subject.

In this regard there were times when consideration had to be given to the problem of supply and communications with the Pacific seaboard of Canada. Prior to 1885, when the Canadian Pacific Railway (C.P.R.) was completed, the only connection was via the stormy seas of Cape Horn or across the Panama isthmus, which was dominated by America. This major rail development shortened the supply route between East and West by nearly three months. From a strategic point of view it was of significant importance because previously orders to ships had to be taken round the southern tip of the continent which was a great disadvantage. Thus, when, in 1886, the Nanaimo and Esquimalt Railway, an extension of the C.P.R., linking the coal port of Nanaimo with Esquimalt, was opened, the support facilities were virtually complete.

Nevertheless there still remained Britain's final requirement for a communication link with the Far East via Canada and this was subsequently met by a fast C.P.R. mail ship service from Vancouver to Australia and Hong Kong via Japan; if necessary these Royal mail ships (EMPRESS OF INDIA, EMPRESS OF CHINA and EMPRESS OF JAPAN) could be converted into armed merchant cruisers in time of war thus meeting the commercial and strategic needs of the Empire; the eventual laying of a trans-Pacific submarine cable in 1902 completed the system for fast transmission of information around the globe.

A rough sketch plan of Esquimalt Naval Base, as at 1903 showing the positions of many of the installations, is provided under Appendix V.

Having taken passage across the Atlantic to Canada, the journey to Vancouver on the West Coast took Bickford some days. Although it was something of an experience, with spectacular views when travelling through the Rocky Mountains on a train sometimes requiring two engines to cope with the steep gradients, the Rear Admiral was anxious to get to his destination as soon as possible and get on with his new job.

From Vancouver he had a further journey to Victoria where the Naval base at Esquimalt was situated on the outskirts of the city. On arrival, with his wife and eldest daughter, Rear Admiral Bickford took up residence at his new home which he was to occupy when ashore for the next three years.

H.M.S. Warspite

The usual courtesy calls were made on the Lieutenant Governor of British Columbia, the Mayor of Victoria, the United States Consul etc. and then his Naval duties became his main preoccupation.

The flagship, H.M.S. WARSPITE, commanded by Captain Colin Keppel D.S.O. Royal Navy, was a coal burning, military rigged armoured cruiser of about 8400 tons with a speed of 16 knots. She had been completed in June 1888 at Chatham Dockyard and had a compliment of 555 Officers and men.

Her armament consisted of four newly designed 9.2 inch breech loading guns, ten 6 inch breech loaders, four 6 pounders, sixteen smaller guns and six 18 inch torpedo tubes. She was one of only two ships in the Navy, the other being H.M.S. IMPERIEUSE, to have their main armament on four positions, fore and aft and on either side; an idea taken from the French. Originally these ships were designed to utilise auxiliary sail power for distant cruising but this was found to be uneconomical and accordingly the idea was abandoned. They were the last armoured ships where there was an attempt to apply sail; it was a time of radical change and the Admiralty found it difficult to accept a Navy without sail power, particularly as early steam engines were unreliable.

In any event this class of ship was not considered to be a great success but with improvements they were turned into useful flagships.

Rear Admiral Bickford hoisted his flag in 'WARSPITE' on Thursday 13th December 1900. During her commission on the Station she was engaged in essential if seemingly unspectacular operations mainly consisting of exercises and cruises in the waters off the North and South American coasts.

The work of the Squadron as can be seen was a matter of ensuring that communications and trade were protected when the Empire was widely extended; this was similar to the operations undertaken by Bickford in the Far East and among the Islands of the Western Pacific.

In fact relations with the United States were particularly strained at the time because the United States considered Northern waters, and especially those of the Bering Sea, to be under her sole jurisdiction quite apart from a long standing dispute with Britain over Alaskan boundaries when gold discoveries in the Yukon were made.

These matters had come to a head, when in 1886 Canadian schooners on a sealing expedition were seized by an American revenue cutter in the Bering Sea. Britain, the protecting Power, protested that the Sea was open and that this was a flagrant violation of International Law; she won her case some years later at a tribunal in Paris, and Canadian sealing interests received compensation.

However the dispute in 1888 became so serious that at one stage it nearly led to war and British and American warships patrolled the seas from which sealing ships were excluded.

The situation was such that an attack on Esquimalt by United States cruisers was considered possible at a time when its defences were relatively weak. While it is true that some minor effort to increase the number of ships in the Squadron, during the period 1890-1903, was being made by way of the arrival of two Torpedo Boat Destroyers (T.B.D.'s) 'SPARROWHAWK' and 'VIRAGO' in 1897, they represented but a small contribution towards meeting overall needs. Nonetheless, these boats were quite challenging. They were built by Laird's of Birkenhead, of 300 tons each, twin-screw, with 6200 horsepower engines giving a speed of 30 knots and armed with quick firing guns. Of sleek appearance with a low forecastle, four funnels and painted black for night attack, they looked very formidable. With a compliment of 58 officers and ratings and carrying 80 tons of coal they represented a powerful deterrent. The two craft remained on the Station for six years before moving on to the China Station in 1904.

During this period of uncertainty it became necessary for two or three Royal Navy ships to go on patrol together leaving the remainder behind at the base for its protection.

In these circumstances Rear Admiral Bickford quickly came to realise the weakness of his Squadron when compared with the United States naval forces; he had only eight ships of consequence against the whole of their

Torpedo Boat Destroyers ‘Virago’ and ‘Sparrowhawk’, Esquimalt, 1901

considerable fleet. He complained bitterly to the Admiralty about the situation but it was of no avail and he was told that European and Chinese Stations had greater demands for ships.

However, when later, an 'entente cordiale' with the United States appeared to be the best way of proceeding, Bickford's diplomatic skill was well demonstrated by way of the fact that, following his numerous earlier visits to neighbouring American ports, he had become quite friendly with the Admiral commanding the United States fleet; as evidence of this he became Godfather to one of his children.

Nevertheless, Bickford was still particularly concerned and let it be known that in a crisis, perhaps involving the Alaska boundary or the Panama Canal, his Squadron would be quite incapable of dealing with it in the face of vastly superior naval forces. If there was confrontation, American demands would undoubtedly have to be met but the Board of Admiralty in London seemed unwilling to face up to the position.

Meantime the flagship continued with what appeared to be somewhat mundane work. The new Commander-in-Chief was by now well established and the Squadron was engaged in demonstrating such a show of strength as was possible in the circumstances. Then, amid her normal routine, 'WARSPITE' suddenly became the backdrop to a Royal visit to Esquimalt by the Duke and Duchess of York (later King George V and Queen Mary) on 1st October 1901.

Originally the visit had been scheduled to occur at Victoria but the Duke telegraphed Bickford to say that he wanted it to take place at Esquimalt, perhaps because he was rather keen on the Navy.

The Commander-in-Chief, his wife, son and daughter were to entertain the Royal party to lunch on board 'WARSPITE' and naturally this exercise involved a great deal of preparation and all the ships in the Squadron had to look at their best which meant that much of the ships company's time had to be given over to spit and polish.

On the day, the Royal guests drove in an open carriage through the streets of Victoria to Esquimalt with much public acclaim. A mounted escort was provided by the North West Mounted Police from the Outer Wharf of the City where the Royal party had landed earlier from the white painted R.M.S. EMPRESS OF INDIA which had been converted for use as a Royal Yacht. She had steamed from Vancouver City, where the party had arrived by Royal Train, escorted by 'AMPHION', 'PHAETON', 'CONDOR' and 'SPARROWHAWK' with Fisheries Protection Steamer 'QUADRA' also in attendance. On arrival at Esquimalt and after making a cursory inspection of the ships of the Squadron, which were dressed overall, the Royal party sat down to lunch on board the flagship where they remained for about an hour and a half. The menu, as illustrated, seems to have been quite varied and comprehensive while the table must have looked very splendid when set with the best silver, china, and glass.

While the visit did not last very long the Duke and Duchess seemed well pleased with their reception and with the arrangements that had been made; for this and for his general good work the Rear Admiral was commended by his guests. The Duke and Duchess then returned to Victoria where they were provided with accommodation which had been specially prepared for them at the Mount Baker Hotel; they used the hotel for the remainder of their stay in Victoria. The Royal tour was continued on Thursday 3rd October 1901 when they left Vancouver by train to travel eastwards.

In truth everyone was quite relieved when the visit was over and normal work could be resumed. The ship's routine was subsequently carried on in an orderly manner and the Commander-in-Chief continued to undertake his duties with great seriousness. For instance, it is recorded that he was obliged to write to the Lieutenant Governor on 15th October 1901 about 'the promiscuous use of firearms in the neighbourhood of the Royal Naval Hospital'. It seems that the Captain of H.M.S. AMPHION, a steel cruiser of 4300 tons, had complained to the Commander-in-Chief that two rifle bullets had struck the ship, one just missing a sailor and the other striking the funnel, while the ship was at her mooring - a bullet was enclosed! It was pointed out that this was a serious matter and a dangerous practice. The shots had apparently come from near the Hudson Bay Storehouse so perhaps it was a case of someone trying out a new rifle.

H. M. S. WARSPITE.

1st October 1901.

Potage.

Consommé

Filets de saumon à la belle vue.

Cotelettes d'agneau aux petits pois.

Chaudfroid coq de bruyère à la russe.

Galantine de dindon à l'aspic

Poulet à la Béchamel

Pâtés de gibier

Quartier d'agneau roti.

Boeuf à la jardinière.

Jambon à la Yorke. Langues de boeufs.

Macedoine de fruits. Gelée au vin

Charlotte Russe. Pâtés à jejune

Crême à la graise. Crême à l'ananas.

Oeufs à la Dauphine. Sandwiches à la caviare

Creme de Framboise Glacé

The Menu for Luncheon for The Duke and Duchess of York on Board H.M.S. Warspite, 1st, October, 1901

By now 'WARSPITE' had been on the Station for some time and she was due to return to Britain where she would join the Reserve. Accordingly, after a send-off she left Esquimalt, early in March 1902, sailing southwards on her long voyage home; on the way she would rendezvous with H.M.S. GRAFTON, her replacement.

H.M.S. GRAFTON was a more modern Cruiser of 7350 tons, with a speed of 20 knots carrying a compliment of 560 Officers and men, which had been completed at Blackwall in 1894. Her armament consisted of two 9.2 inch guns, ten 6 inch Quick Firing guns, twelve 6 pounders, five 3 pounders, seven maxim guns and four torpedo tubes; quite a formidable array of weaponry. There were eight similar cruisers in her class, making up a powerful string of warships.

'GRAFTON's' commission on this occasion was for three years and it had begun earlier in January 1902 at Chatham where her ships company had marched along the jetty from the accommodation hulk, H.M.S. PEMBROKE, to join the ship under the command of Captain John Marx Royal Navy.

On 22nd January she had left South Lock Chatham Dockyard to anchor off Sheerness. Two days later her journey to the Pacific began in earnest.

After coaling at Plymouth, there was a rough crossing to Madeira after which the ship proceeded to St. Vincent in the West Indies and then on to Montevideo in South America. The next leg of the trip, at fourteen knots, was to be via the Straits of Magellan at the southern tip of South America where the weather round Cape Horn is always stormy and the seas at their most violent. To reduce the length of the journey 'GRAFTON' used the quicker route through Smyths Straits to the Pacific. Her next stop was Valparaiso in Chile where a 21 gun salute was fired for the Government and it was reciprocated by shore batteries. Further up the coast was Coquimbo, a small rather dingy town, where the two ships were to take on coal and exchange roles.

On March 22nd 1902, Rear Admiral Bickford transferred his flag to 'GRAFTON' and Captain Colin Keppel D.S.O. Royal Navy assumed command of the ship when Captain John Marx Royal Navy, took H.M.S. WARSPITE home to Britain. H.M.S. GRAFTON then continued her voyage northwards calling at San Jose de Guatemala, the port for the Capital city in the hills above. A force of sailors from the ship was prepared to land to enforce the payment of a British Government debt but fortunately its use was unnecessary. A few days later the ship survived an earthquake tremor which gave her quite a shaking and the shock was severe enough to kill a large number of people ashore.

After taking on coal 'GRAFTON' continued her passage to the north skirting Acapulco and the United States ports of Santa Monica and San Diego where a call had to be made with the intention of landing two midshipmen for hospital treatment, as they were suffering from fever. Sadly one of them died before reaching hospital and he had to be buried ashore.

After remaining in harbour for some days and taking on coal, the ship left for Esquimalt, the voyage taking five days. On 8th May 1902 she arrived, having passed through the narrow channel at the harbour entrance leaving Fisquard lighthouse on the port side. On the opposite side of the harbour a red brick signal tower stood out as a landmark on Grant Knoll adjoining the dockyard. It had been constructed at the instigation of Rear Admiral Bickford and was named after him. The tower is an attractive octagonal building, 50 feet high, resembling a small lighthouse with the words 'Bickford Tower 1901' inscribed over the entrance.

It had been constructed as a lookout position for the purpose of communicating with vessels outside the harbour entrance when they were seeking permission to enter; more importantly it upgraded harbour defences, without major funding, by giving the appearance of stronger fortifications to any potential enemy.

The building was designed by Thomas Woodgate, a civil engineer, within the offices and employment of the Royal Navy; he was designated 'Officer in charge of works' and some of the other substantial buildings at the base are also attributed to him.

The tower is approached from the dockyard over rocky ground filled in with

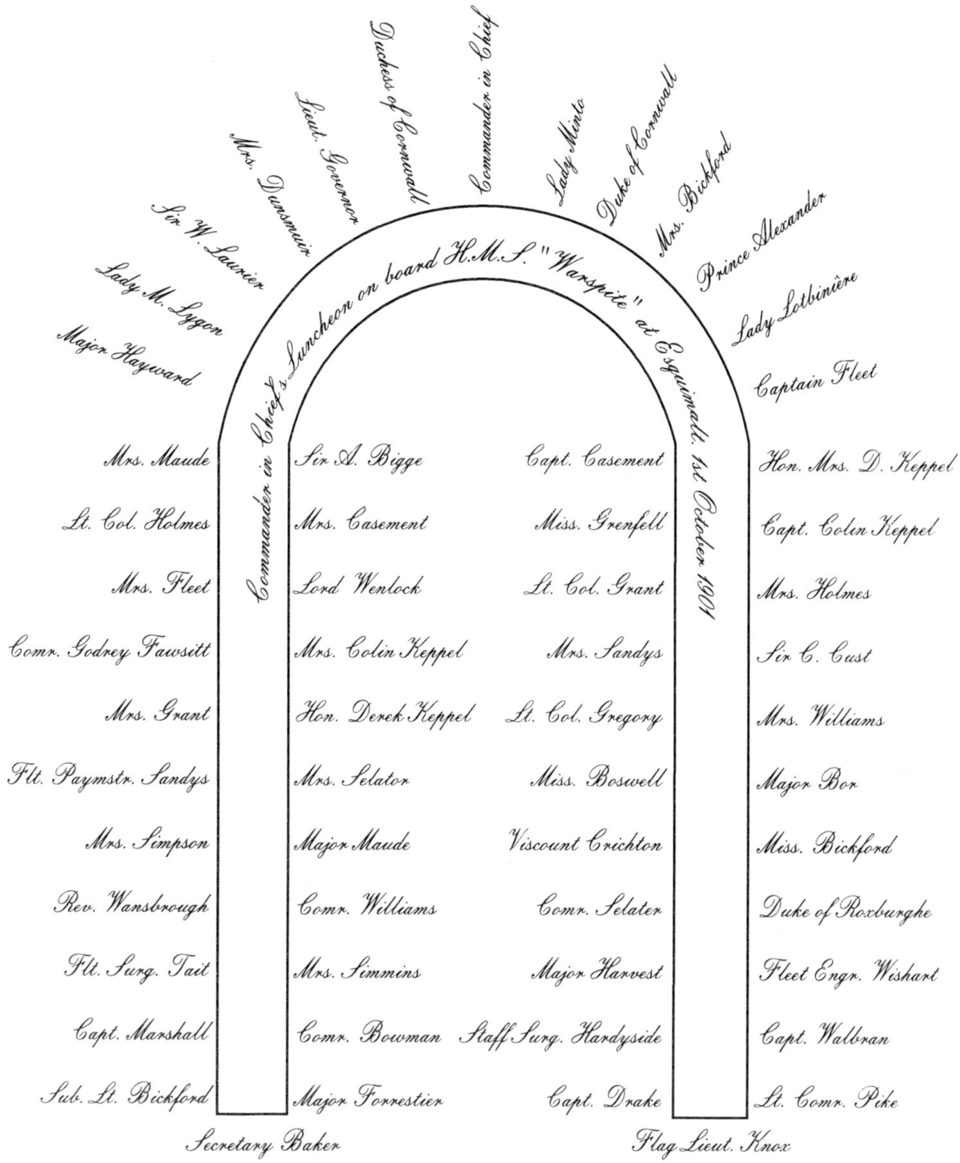

Table Plan for Luncheon, held for Duke and Duchess of York on board H.M.S. Warspite, Esquimalt, 1st October, 1901

rubble which supports an inclined timber walkway to the entrance.

The interior of the building is made up of four floor levels, each approached by wooden stairs.

On the ground floor there is a W/T office which housed morse code equipment etc. There is also a stove on this level providing heat by way of vents to the floors above to prevent condensation; light enters the building through openings with windows at each floor level.

Mounting to the first storey there is a mess room for watchkeepers, lookouts and signalmen, having a sink, stove and room for a table and chairs; an officers' room adjoins. Rising to the stage above there is an equipment store for signal lamps, flags and pennants etc.

The signal room at the top of the tower, similar to the lamp-room of a lighthouse, is reached by stairs with a hatchway to one side. It is a particularly well lit area having tall glazed windows to all sides under a white painted conical roof. Double doors lead to a surrounding galleried platform providing a lookout position with views over the base and anchorage to the open sea beyond.

There are fixings for a heavy signal mast used for the hoisting of flags and lamps at night to indicate whether it was permissable for incoming ships to enter the harbour. In addition there are supports for a semaphore post. Manual semaphore flags were frequently used to communicate easily between ships and shore providing confidentiality of messages. An advancement in this method of signalling was the introduction of a mechanical transmitter by way of a pole having pivotal arms instead of flags at its top, which were operated by handles at the base. The device was invented by a Colonel Palsey, stationed at Chatham, Kent, and used in Napoleonic times to the extent that a series of signal towers were established between London and Portsmouth so that the Admiralty could communicate rapidly with the fleet.

Considering all its facilities, the tower at Esquimalt represented quite a sophisticated early warning system for its day, and still proudly stands at the entrance of the harbour as a tribute to its originator and to its architect.

It is interesting that Vice Admiral Sir Cyprian Bridge G.C.B. visited the Commander-in-Chief on 25th May 1902 as a friend and guest on his way to take up his appointment as Commander-in-Chief, China Station and to fly his flag in H.M.S. GLORY; he would take passage to Hong Kong in R.M.S. EMPRESS OF JAPAN.

He had known Esquimalt in his earlier days when he had paid a visit there as a midshipman in H.M.S. BRISK. He was particularly interested in naval defence on a world-wide basis and he had written a number of papers on the subject including one in support of maintaining Esquimalt and the strengthening of its defences. Doubtless a discussion took place between the two men regarding such matters and the newly built Bickford Tower must have been of particular relevance.

In the early days, Esquimalt, providing a fine anchorage and a new graving dock, was connected to Victoria, about four miles distant, by a tramway. There were, by this time, various naval buildings at the base besides a sports ground and the hospital, though the residential area was little more than a village with a single street.

The Squadron itself consisted of three cruisers, a sloop, a destroyer, two torpedo boats, two T.B.D's, a store ship and various other small craft though the total number of vessels varied according to the completion of their individual commissions.

On arrival 750 tons of coal were taken on board 'GRAFTON' and shore leave was given. In subsequent days there were sports competitions and regattas besides exercises and the testing of the ship's armament and her torpedoes.

King Edward VII's Coronation was due to take place on June 25th but it had to be delayed owing to his illness. Nevertheless the day was celebrated with twenty four hours leave and by 'Splicing the Mainbrace' with a double rum ration but the shore activities had to be postponed until a later date.

The Bickford Tower, Esquimalt B.C., Canada
(With permission of J. and M. Penney)

There followed a cruise to Nanoose Bay, Comox and Duncan Bay where the officers went on a salmon fishing expedition up the Campbell River. Other remote places visited on the cruise included Drew Harbour, Indian Mission Bay and Telegraph Bay.

On returning to Esquimalt the remainder of the Squadron had assembled for the delayed Coronation celebrations. On 9th August 1902 a 21 gun salute was fired and the ships were dressed overall. 'GRAFTON' was opened to inspection by the public which gave people a rare opportunity to see for themselves at close quarters the workings of a warship. It was always immensely popular. In the evening there was a firework display and the ships were illuminated with necklaces of electric lamps to outline their shapes which was altogether very spectacular.

During the following weeks the daily routine mainly consisted of gunnery exercises with target practice and small arms competitions besides normal seamanship evolutions.

In December after the interminable intake of coal the ship began a cruise southwards having already been in dry dock to have her hull scraped. 'Coaling Ship' was a filthy and miserable task which had to be frequently undertaken. Targets for time taken were set to encourage the ships company supported by the officers to complete and operation as quickly as possible; afterwards they had to spend a good deal of time cleaning up the ship and themselves.

In the course of her next cruise, the ship made visits to the American ports of Monterey and San Diego, which were always favoured. Then, setting a southerly course, she sailed at economical speed towards the coast of Mexico, where at Mazatlan, a 21 gun salute was fired for the country's President.

Later in the month, preparations were made for Christmas and on the day itself, after Church on the Quarterdeck, the Admiral, with his wife and daughter, toured the mess decks and sampled the Christmas fare. In the evening there was a sing song but as the temperature was so high due to the tropical heat everybody spent a great deal of time trying to find the coolest place in the ship.

The next stop en route was San Jose de Guatamala where shark fishing took place and a small fish was caught by one of the ships company, much to the surprise of those watching.

While in harbour the ship was repainted in French grey after her yellow and white livery. Visits to Guatemala City were arranged for the ships company who took the railway which carried passengers up the mountain to the city above which stood at over 4000 feet.

She continued on course southwards to Nicaragua, Colombia and Panama where the Canal project was being considered at that time. Visits were arranged at the Peruvian ports of Payta and Callao where several old Peruvian warships without engines or guns were anchored. They had been laid up after an earlier War between Chile and Peru and under the peace agreement they were not to be used for ten years. The undertaking was coming to an end and the ships were being repaired for renewed use.

Whilst there, the Peruvian capital, Lima, high up in the mountains above the port, about forty miles distant, was visited by members of 'GRAFTON's' ships company.

She then took on board 1123 tons of coal, the greatest quantity of the commission. On the ensuing voyage she hit an object which shook the ship and turned out to be a whale which she had killed and impaled on her bow ram. It was eventually dislodged and she proceeded without further difficulty.

The busy Chilean port of Valparaiso was reached shortly afterwards and it was seen that two of that country's battleships lay at anchor. Salutes were exchanged which was particularly appropriate as the Admiral of the Chilean Navy was a retired Commander from the Royal Navy!

The farthest port south which was reached was Corral. Valdivia township was visited by the Admiral who was taken there in his steam barge, fifteen miles up river.

On the return journey to Esquimalt, Coquimbo was again visited and races were arranged for the ships whalers and cutters. Coal was taken on board at many of the ports of call and the Cocos Islands were sighted. In 1897 Rear Admiral Palliser of the Pacific Station, who seems to have been quite a character, took his flagship H.M.S. IMPERIEUSE on a treasure hunting expedition to the Islands which were under the flag of Costa Rica. It was believed that the Peruvian State treasure had been buried there but in spite of all his efforts to find it, Palliser had no success. Still undaunted he continued his quest in his own steamship 'LYTTON' in 1903 but still he found nothing. Finally, in 1905, in company with Earl Fitzwilliam, he set off in the yacht 'VERONIQUE' to the Islands but to his chagrin he found that, a Mr Harold Gray with a party, was already there having had permission from the Costa Rican Government; accordingly Palliser had to abandon his expedition. In fact there is no record of anyone ever finding any treasure on the Islands. It seems doubtful whether the Admiralty ever found out about these adventures either, as Palliser continued to achieve promotion before finally retiring in 1904 as a full Admiral.

On arrival at Esquimalt the ship went into dry dock for maintenance and sadly whilst it was there two sailors fell forty feet into the dock and one of them was killed. A funeral for him was arranged and he was buried with full military honours, the gun carriage being manned by his messmates.

The ship came out of dock shortly afterwards, was re-coaled and proceeded southwards for another visit to San Francisco to attend the celebrations for the visit of President Theodore Roosevelt to California. On the way a stoker fell into the sea but was rescued by the Officer of the Watch who dived in after him fully clothed.

On arrival 'GRAFTON' joined no less than eight American warships in the harbour beyond the Golden Gate. The ships were decked out with flags and illuminated by night and 'GRAFTON' was open to visitors. As the President reviewed the ships the ships companies manned the sides, the bands played the National Anthem and 21 gun salutes were fired.

Only petty officers were given overnight shore leave; the remainder of the ships company being denied this privilege for fear of desertion in a port which was tempting from a work point of view with jobs advertised on placards.

'GRAFTON' sailed for Esquimalt two days later and on arrival, there was a regatta and sports at Beacon Hill and on 26th June 1903 the King's Birthday was celebrated with a march through the town by the blue jackets and Marines with a battery of field guns. The Lieutenant Governor of British Columbia, Sir Henry Joly de Lotbinière K.C.M.G., accompanied by Rear Admiral Bickford took the salute and a seven gun salute was fired by the field battery. Captain Keppel led three cheers for the King.

It seems that celebrations of this kind were commonplace between cruises when firing at targets and the testing of torpedoes etc. took place. Apart from these activities, sports and sailing regattas were perpetually being held. Fishing expeditions, particularly up the Campbell River by the officers, together with shooting parties also took up much of the time. On one occasion a young bear was brought on board as a mascot and named 'Jim' by the ships company. A sailor was detailed off to look after the animal which must have had a pretty miserable existence; it is not recorded what became of the poor beast.

After a few days in harbour at Esquimalt, 'GRAFTON' left for torpedo practice near the ammunition magazine on Cole Island. Lying off shore was a private sailing ship 'COLUMBIA' whose crew let off distress rockets to celebrate the skipper's birthday but unfortunately some landed ashore and flames in the woods could be seen.

Fire engines from ashore and equipment from the ship were summoned as soon as it was discovered that the fire was at Captain Keppel's house. This was a rather smart timber bungalow which was burnt to the ground and a total ruin; unfortunately it was not insured and history does not reveal whether the owner ever secured any compensation.

A few weeks later the Commander-in-Chief inspected 'GRAFTON' and observed gunnery practice and torpedo runs after which he sent a complimentary signal to the officers and ships company in respect of their fine performance. Subsequently the ship undertook speed trials in which she

Patrol frigate H.M.C.S. Calgary, leaving harbour passing the Bickford Tower, Esquimalt
(By courtesy of the Canadian Forces)

attained 18.5 knots in a choppy swell which was considered to be the equivalent of 21 knots in calmer waters and altogether represented a very satisfactory performance.

A draft of 100 men arrived from England for the base and most went to 'GRAFTON' to cover vacancies through ill health, time expired men and desertions of which there were a few.

The following week the most memorable, but unfortunate, episode of the whole commission occurred. One of the cruisers in the Squadron, H.M.S. FLORA, which had left harbour for target practice went aground on rocks, in fog, off Comox.

At the time 'GRAFTON' was in dock for maintenance with all her gear removed. There was a great hurried effort to get her ready for sea and to take coal on board. Dockyard equipment with pumps, hawsers and hoists were loaded on to a lighter for towing, with two other lighters attached to either side of the ship. Within an amazingly short space of time the ship left on her 120 mile journey to the wrecked 'FLORA'.

On arrival it was observed that the cruiser, with a heavy list to port, was lying across a rocky promontory with her bows on the beach and her quarterdeck at water level; her after funnel was completely submerged.

It seems that she had just taken on board the maximum tonnage of coal, about 800-900 tons, at the Union Coaling Station and after sailing two or three miles she was suddenly enveloped in fog while proceeding at about 10 knots. At the moment that she had to turn into the channel she ran onto the rocks and her bows became jammed in a crevice.

The only way to dislodge and tow her off was to pump out her stern as quickly as possible. Accordingly her coal had to be removed and wire hawser attached so that a pull could take place on the next full tide after 'GRAFTON' had anchored ahead of the wreck. At the first attempt the cables parted so all eight 4.7 inch guns had to be removed and loaded on to the lighter; a massive task.

Then all her stores, ammunition and torpedoes had to be removed. On the second attempt she only moved about six feet so finally the Commander-in-Chief ordered the several hundred tons of coal remaining to be taken out of her bunkers together with the forward 6 inch gun, weighing seven tons, and all her anchors.

After all this work had been completed the tow was repeated and this time the ship slid into deep water. Collision mats were placed in position over the damaged area and the hull was slowly towed back to Esquimalt. On arrival 'FLORA' was manoeuvred into dry dock. The officers and ships companies of the ships involved in the salvage operation were commended for all their good work by the Commander-in-Chief.

A Court of Enquiry was immediately established and this confirmed that the Captain and Navigating Officer of 'FLORA' were to be court martialled the following day on board 'GRAFTON'.

Although Rear Admiral Bickford's relief, Commodore Goodrich M.V.O. Royal Navy, had arrived whilst he was away on this operation and was already flying his broad pennant, the Admiralty sent a signal instructing the Commander-in-Chief to remain in command until the Court Martial had been completed. In these circumstances the pennant had to be replaced by Bickford's flag on a temporary basis.

The Court-martial resulted in both of 'FLORA's' officers being severely reprimanded for hazarding their ship and they were cautioned to take more care in the future.

The following Monday on 21st December 1903, Rear Admiral Bickford finally struck his flag and the Commodore's broad pennant was at last hoisted. The Commander-in-Chief and his Secretary left for Seattle with Captain Keppel who had made a short speech to the ships company. During the period of his command of 'GRAFTON', she had fired 58 salutes and called at more than 60 places.

Captain Keppel C.B. D.S.O. was appointed, at a later date, as Captain of the Royal Yacht 'VICTORIA AND ALBERT' and a letter of congratulation

H.M.S. Gafton, 1902
(From a watercolour by W. J. Sutton)

was sent to him by Rear Admiral Bickford.

Thus ended a period of mixed fortunes for the Commander-in-Chief. He was now looking forward to a spell of leave back in England although he was fortunate to have had some members of his family with him while in command; these included his wife and eldest daughter who accompanied him on two cruises along the South American coast, while his son, the author's father, was serving as a Lieutenant in the flagship at the time.

Rear Admiral Bickford was the last officer of this rank to command ships on the Pacific Station. Commodore Goodrich M.V.O. took over command of the second class cruiser, H.M.S. BONADVENTURE, in 1903 as his flagship, and Captain Robert Grant Royal Navy took 'GRAFTON' home to Portsmouth and then Sherness where she was paid off in 1904.

So far as the base was concerned after 1905 it became of minimal use, with Commander A.T. Hunt Royal Navy in H.M.S. SHEARWATER as its first officer-in-charge; in 1910 it was handed over to the fledgling Royal Canadian Navy.

CHAPTER VI

RETIREMENT

Rear Admiral Bickford did not manage to get home in time to spend the Christmas of 1903 in England as the journey from British Columbia took sometime. However he arrived early in the New Year.

It is said that one of his usual customs when he had been away at sea was to line up his children, as though he was taking Divisions on the Quarterdeck, and then enquire of his wife how they had behaved while he had been away. If the report was unsatisfactory for any of them they were for the high jump!

On this occasion his leave was all the more enjoyable because on 10th February 1904 he received promotion to Vice Admiral and received the Admiralty's thanks for "the manner in which you performed important duties which devolved on you during the period of your command".

His next and final appointment was to the Royal Naval College at Greenwich where for the month of June he gave a course of instruction to Flag Officers on the subject of Strategy and Tactics; this was completed on 27th June 1904.

From this stage onwards he busied himself with occasional Admiralty matters although he was virtually unemployed. Nevertheless his pay was probably sufficient to take care of a reasonable standard of living but with a sizeable family, the house in Western Parade, Southsea, was becoming less suitable. Moreover he had in mind his future retirement which was more or less compulsory at the age of 65. Accordingly he decided that a country life would be more appropriate after the countless years spent in a Naval environment; after all he was now 60 years of age.

So it was that, after looking around the nearby countryside, at last he found a property, The Grange, off the High Street in the East Sussex town of Uckfield. It was a typical Victorian Villa in stucco under a slated roof suitable for a gentleman of his standing. There were three or four reception rooms with about six bedrooms to accommodate the children; four of them were now grown up but three were still in their teens.

His eldest son, Andrew, born in 1869, had already left home to make a life overseas. Having met a girl from Guatemala, possibly through an introduction by his father, he left England to marry her and to make a successful life for himself as a banker in Central America. It seems that his father and grandfather had probably encouraged him to look to a career overseas after being told about various places they had visited on the coasts of Central and South America.

It is appropriate that today the Admiral's Sword and decorations should be in the possession of Andrew's descendants living in Guatemala, of whom there are now over thirty in number living near to Guatemala City.

His second son, Arthur, born in 1870, joined the Indian Army and rose to the rank of Major in the 56th Rifles before being killed in Mesopotamia in the First World War; he had failed entry to the Royal Navy much to his father's disappointment.

His third son, John ('Jack'), born in 1879 (my father) went into the Royal Navy which gave the Admiral undoubted pleasure and an outline of his career is given in subsequent pages.

His fourth son, Maurice, born in 1888, also joined the Indian Army, partly because of his elder brother's enlistment and partly because the pay was better than in the British Army. He rose to the rank of Lieutenant Colonel in the 17th Dogra Regiment.

On retirement he returned to Britain and went to live at Murrayfield, in his wife's home city of Edinburgh where he found much of interest and where there were opportunities for golf and fishing.

His fifth and youngest son, Francis ('Frank'), born in 1889, entered the Priesthood and won a Military Cross in the First World War. He subsequently became President of St. Edmunds College, Ware, Herefordshire, a Seminary and Public School, which post he held for fourteen years. As a Monsignor and Vicar General he died in London in 1968.

Of the Admiral's daughters, the eldest, Marie, born in 1875, accompanied her father and mother in British Columbia when he was Commander-in-Chief. She married a Dutchman and following his death continued to live in Holland throughout World War II where she assisted Allied airmen who were shot down; she finally died aged over 100.

His second daughter, Winifride ('Wintz') born in 1886, married a Captain in the Royal Engineers and in her retirement and final years lived in Hove and Lewes, Sussex; she lies buried next to her parents at Herons Ghyll, a few miles north of Uckfield.

Whilst living at The Grange before the First World War, life was not without its humorous moments. For instance on one notable occasion, Frank, decided that it would be fun, when his parents were entertaining guests to dinner downstairs, to attempt to empty the bath with a water pistol! The results can be imagined and when the ladies retired after dinner they had a little paddling to do in the entrance hall. The Admiral was not amused and the punishment can be imagined, in spite of his wife's pleas for mercy.

On another occasion, Jack, having been given a toy pistol which fired small arrows with rubber suction tips found it quite amusing to fire at all manner of objects around the house until a misdirected shot in the Morning Room shattered the window - again a heavy price had to be paid!

However times were usually more tranquil and the family was quite close though a fairly strict regime seems to have prevailed; those who had been away were welcomed home and their father was always interested in the way they were getting on in the world.

On 22nd March 1908 at the age of 64, a year before compulsory retirement, he received promotion to the rank of full Admiral to provide some recognition of his past achievements. Admiral Bickford now decided that, without a real job to do, the time had come to finally retire from the Royal Navy.

On 12th May 1908, having received confirmation from the Admiralty that he had been placed on the Retired List and the Auditor General to the Navy had confirmed a Pension of £950 a year, he closed the naval chapter of his life.

It must be said that he only secured his pension after being placed on a list of candidates awaiting a vacancy for a pension and subject to Admiralty approval. While this is confirmed in his private papers his Service Record states that he received a Naval Pension of £150 on 19th January 1912 so this may have represented an additional payment to him as a full Admiral.

On retirement a new life awaited this man who had overcome many trials and tribulations in his career but first he had to survive a devastating blow. In 1910 his wife Kathleen now aged 60 developed what was said to be gout in her left foot which turned to blood poisoning - a Doctor was called from Brighton but could not help and he suggested that the foot should be amputated to prevent the infection from spreading. This was duly carried out but the shock of the operation was such that it led to her death within a few days.

The Admiral was very saddened at the loss of his wife and companion of forty two years and it took him some time to recover. However, he eventually decided to apply himself to work in the community as a distraction from the gap which had opened up in his life.

In due course he was appointed a Justice of the Peace and sat on the Bench in Sussex in addition to carrying out the duties of a Land Tax Commissioner for the County which he diligently performed for the ensuing twenty years. At home he carried on with the help of his daughters and one or two servants.

He became engrossed in his work and as a conscientious member of the Bench he became a well known member of the local community. However as the years took their toll eventually he was forced to give up. Now in his eighty's he spent a good deal of his time contemplating his long passed active service days when the gentle breeze of the Southern Ocean filled his sails and cooled his heated brow.

Eventually, on 9th October 1927, having moved to live near to his daughter in Hove he died quietly at home.

He now lies peacefully, next to the grave of his beloved wife, beneath the yew trees in the quiet little graveyard at Herons Ghyll near Uckfield on the fringes of Ashdown Forest.

CHAPTER VII

A SAILOR OF SOME CONSEQUENCE ?

The story is told but what of the man.

His great nephew can recollect how, as a schoolboy, he was given a 10/- note when he visited the Admiral; it was a great deal of money at that time and the gift made a lasting impression on the recipient.

The only other person who could recall his last years, was the Reverend Mother of the convent school at the small town in Sussex where he retired - she could remember him as a benign old gentleman who slowly took his daily walk passing the shops, deep in thought.

Accordingly, he must be judged from what knowledge we have of his life and actions; these are substantially documented but they must be taken within the context of conditions prevailing at the time.

Some would say that in later life he came to rule like a martinet while others can detect a more gentle streak in his character which shone through as instanced by his concern for the prisoners of the NISERO and the natives of Samoa - one letter from a couple there talks of admiration for him and with great affection. It alludes to presents they have sent to him which took the form of "fans and tappias (cloths), also one water melon and a basket of mangoes besides pine apples".

As he was leaving Apia, the letter asks him to send another photograph as "his friends" wanted to hang up two, side by side.

It goes on to say "Indeed Captain we are exceedingly proud and feel ourselves illustrious at the thought of having come in contact with such a gentleman as you are - not only because of your position but because of your ways and speech; all so pleasant and pleasing to the ear. Yes indeed, we have missed a friend but such are the ups and downs of life."

This correspondence epitomises the goodwill that was generally expressed by the inhabitants of Samoa towards the Captain of 'KATOOMBA' in spite of the firm action he was obliged to take.

The collection of cowrie, mother-of-pearl and other shells, which he received as gifts and brought home, give substance to this fact.

Nevertheless it cannot be denied that his early training and the strict discipline instilled into him as a gunnery officer influenced not only his private life but also his command of men. In this respect his actions both at home and in the service of his country were driven by a sense of duty. It must be remembered that he had participated in, and lived through, some of the most dramatic changes that had taken place within the long history of the Royal Navy - changes from sail to steam and in the construction of ships and their armament - thus it can be seen that demands on the man in respect of courage were not inconsiderable and it could be said that he represented an above average example of a Victorian naval officer.

We know he was both concise and something of a stickler for detail, as his reports clearly indicate; in addition, he was resourceful and undoubtedly he had a natural skill in diplomacy. However there is one matter which, to the layman, often seems strange and it concerns the reason why such a distinguished career did not warrant further decoration for services to the Nation.

Admiral Bickford does not appear to have made any substantial mistakes in judgement during the course of his naval life apart from some minor errors in ship handling etc. and certainly he does not seem to have had to survive anything like a reprimand as other successful men had done before and after him.

He received a C.M.G. as a Captain at the comparatively early age of forty-one and of this he was justifiably proud. Additionally he was appointed A.D.C. to Queen Victoria in later years, so it might reasonably have been expected that with such credentials something extra would have been bestowed upon him; for lesser services at that time others received Knighthood's or even greater honours.

It has been suggested that the answer to this question may lie in the general attitude towards those in the Services who did not subscribe to membership of the Established Church in Victorian England.

Although changes were taking place and there was beginning to be an increase in religious tolerance it is a fact that there still remained some antipathy towards Roman Catholics at the time and especially in the Armed Forces.

It has been recorded that latterly in Samoa there had been some discord between the Three Powers and Bickford, probably motivated in part by petty jealousy of his diplomatic success.

Doubtless this aspect of affairs was reported to the Foreign Office, possibly intimating that as a Catholic he had an unfair advantage in his negotiations with Mataafa. This is a matter of speculation and it seems unlikely that history will ever give the complete answer to what is, after all, a small matter in terms of a long and already distinguished life.

Following his death the Admiralty wrote a letter to his family expressing appreciation of his valuable services to the Royal Navy and particularly when he was Commander-in-Chief of the Pacific Station.

However, before concluding, the story would not be complete if something of the active service lives of other members of the family, who followed in the footsteps of this noteworthy sailor, remained unrecorded. Accordingly the ensuing few pages are intended to complete at least some part of that record.

CHAPTER VIII

A TRADITION CARRIED FORWARD

Had Admiral Bickford lived longer, undoubtedly he would have been filled with a sense of pride and pleasure, on hearing that the seafaring traditions of his family were being maintained.

In this regard, from family notes and other sources, it is recorded that no less than 27 members of the family, including close relatives, have served in the Royal Navy over the past two centuries. They have provided 6 Admirals, 9 Captains, 4 Commanders, 1 Fleet Paymaster, 1 Hydrographer, a Surgeon and a Wren; quite a remarkable record.

Some personal experiences in that regard, even in outline, seem worth passing on, in spite of the fact that there are those which are more deserving and noteworthy than others.

For instance there was his son John ("Jack"), my father, to whom reference has already been made, who was given plenty of encouragement by his parents to find out about naval matters during his boyhood when living at Western Parade in Southsea.

Both his mother and father, being deeply involved with the Navy, thought that their third son should become familiar with ships and the Dockyard as they wanted at least one of their children to enter the Service after their elder two sons had chosen other careers.

'Jack's' education was in part provided by Eastmans Naval Academy, located near his home in Southsea, prior to his entry to H.M.S. BRITANNIA moored off Dartmouth in Devonshire. In 1862 she had sailed from Portsmouth, having taken over from H.M.S. ILLUSTRIOUS, to Portland in Dorset under the command of Captain R. Powell Royal Navy. He considered the location unsuitable for her particular work so the following year he sailed her on to her long time home on the River Dart.

Needless to say family celebrations followed Jack's acceptance for the Navy and the donning of his first uniform as a cadet proved to be a rather special event. History seemed to be repeating itself at least in this respect.

After finishing a two year course as a cadet in 'BRITANNIA' he was sent to H.M.S. MAJESTIC to complete his early training at sea.

In 1897 he took passage in H.M.S. ENDYMION to join H.M.S. CENTURION, the flagship of the China Station, as a midshipman where he remained until 1899.

After returning home, he joined the training ship H.M.S. RALEIGH at Devonport and then went on to H.M.S. ST GEORGE in the training squadron, finishing up with a course at the Royal Naval College Greenwich in 1900.

By then, having been promoted to Sub-Lieutenant, he continued to gain experience with further sea time in the destroyer H.M.S. ALBATROSS attached to the Home Fleet.

In the spring of 1901 an appointment to his father's flagship, the cruiser H.M.S. WARSPITE at Esquimalt, B.C., was received. It was greeted with some apprehension as it is often difficult to work under prominent men and particularly when the person concerned is your own father; much is expected but demands are seldom met with complete satisfaction. Moreover it is often necessary to doubly prove yourself before being accepted for your own worth by your fellow officers who probably feel that you are being given an over generous helping hand.

Nevertheless, this period of 'Jack's' career seems to have been reasonably enjoyable not only because of the varied conditions in Canada but also because it gave him the chance of showing his worth when commanding Torpedo Boats Nos 39 and 40 which were attached to the Squadron, as already mentioned; this was probably at the instigation of his father who felt it would provide his son with some experience of the responsibilities involved.

During the summer of 1901, prior to the Royal Visit, cruises were arranged for the torpedo boats along the coast of British Columbia which offered the opportunity of fishing up the rivers and of making hunting trips in the forests. It was a fairly relaxed but exciting time for a young officer; the only incident of note seems to have been an occasion when, on one hunting expedition, someone shot the Captain's dog mistaking it for a bear - not a clever thing to do on any count!

When the Admiral's Flag was transferred to H.M.S. GRAFTON in 1902 a number of fellow officers also went with him including young Bickford who was later promoted to Lieutenant before returning to the United Kingdom to join H.M.S. ROYAL OAK, in the Home Fleet.

During the ensuing years, prior to the First World War, Lieutenant Bickford was appointed to a number of ships which varied in size from battleships to destroyers. As a senior Lieutenant he was given command of some of the lesser vessels, and secured his promotion to Lieutenant Commander in 1910.

Between 1912 and 1915 he served in, or commanded destroyers which formed part of the Grand Fleet which was assembled to face the German High Seas Fleet, in order to prove its supremacy; this resulted in the famous Battle of Jutland at the end of May 1915. 'Jack' hoped that his recent contribution to the war at sea would earn him his 'Brass Hat', like some others but, in spite of a Mention in Despatches, it was not to be.

However in the autumn of 1915 he was appointed to the command of a gunboat, H.M.S. BRAMBLE. She was stationed in the Persian Gulf, which was a war zone, and she operated there until the summer of 1918 after which he returned home.

During the closing months of the war and several beyond 'Jack' concluded his active service days by again commanding destroyers in North Sea waters.

The final years of his first period of service were then completed with work with the Naval Reserves at Liverpool until he retired as a Commander in 1923 at the age of 44. A general reduction in the number of officers required by the Navy following the end of the First War, was taking place and many were pressurised by the Admiralty to seek early retirement; naturally it did not improve general career prospects at that time.

However, years later, after the outbreak of World War II, although in his 60's, he put on uniform again and for a time commanded H.M.S. SEA SERPENT, a Combined Operations shore establishment, at Hayling Island near Portsmouth. After what cannot have been an easy time for him because of his age, he was finally appointed to the Historical section of the Admiralty in December 1944, where for the next eighteen months he was engaged in writing the official Naval History of the War.

There are other members of the family who are also worthy of mention in relation to their lives in the Royal Navy.

Among these there was 'Bicky of the Big Guns'; a larger than life character of sufficient interest to appear on the pages of a boys adventure story book of the late 1920's. The incidents recorded [2.] concerned a certain Commander Bickford Royal Navy, one of the Admiral's cousins who, in the First World War, was put in charge of a battery of naval guns mounted ashore on the coast of Belgium to prevent German ships passing through the Dover Straits. He appears to have undertaken some quite astonishing exploits and was seldom seen without a rum bottle sticking out of his pocket, presumably to help to keep out the cold while watch keeping!

Succeeding generations also provided mariners of note. For instance in

2. 'Evans of the Broke' – autobiography by Admiral Lord Mountevans, Chapter XII, page 104, 1947.

World War II, the Admiral had another cousin, Captain Jack Grant Bickford Royal Navy who, as Captain (D) of a flotilla of destroyers based on the east coast commanded H.M.S. EXPRESS and won the D.S.O. for gallantry during attacks on enemy shipping in the North Sea, but he was sadly killed in her in 1940 when she struck a mine. His Officer of the Watch was the Gunnery Officer at the time and he recalls the last words of Jack Grant which, when mortally wounded, were 'Don't leave me Guns'; the Gunnery Officer was later picked up and lived to relate the incident to a member of the family.

Then, perhaps, and more dramatically, the exploits of Lieutenant Commander Edward Oscar Bickford Royal Navy, should be retold.

Ashore, he was apparently renowned for his enjoyment of wardroom parties and perhaps some of this exuberance overflowed and had a bearing on his life at sea.

As Captain of H.M. Submarine 'SALMON', in a Flotilla commanded by Captain P. Ruck-Keene Royal Navy, he daringly located and torpedoed a German U-boat (U.36) on 12th December 1939; one of the first enemy U-boats of the War to be sunk by a British Submarine.

The following day 'SALMON', continuing her patrol, unexpectedly came across the German liner 'BREMEN', her funnel painted light grey, travelling at high speed.

What a spectacular event it would be to attack and sink the pride of the German mercantile fleet.

However, Admiralty orders at the outbreak of hostilities had emphasised the need for R.N. ships to strictly adhere to international law which demanded that unarmed ships were not to be sunk because of the likelihood of loss of civilian life. Only if a vessel constituted a valid threat could action be taken and even then the law insisted that survivors were to be picked up; not really a feasible possibility for a small ship like a submarine.

Bickford had mixed feelings over these demands but he was conscious of his responsibilities and of the instructions, which as a disciplined officer, he was obliged to obey. Accordingly 'BREMEN' was allowed to pass on her way unharmed probably unaware of her proximity to destruction. For Bickford it was a supreme disappointment that such a prize should have been denied to him.

His discomfort in respect of the matter was, however, alleviated to some extent when a message from the Admiralty confirmed that 'BREMEN' was not to be torpedoed.

With these thoughts in mind the boat continued on her way. The following day at about 10.00 a.m. several ships were observed through the periscope about seven miles distant. Having closed on the vessels, to improve identification, it became clear that they represented a strong force of enemy ships. They appeared to consist of two or three heavy cruisers or even pocket battleships, similar to the 'GRAF SPEE', supported by four cruisers, two of the 'HIPPER' Class, the third being of the 'KOENIGSBERG' Class and the fourth, the 'LEIPZIG'; altogether representing a considerable portion of the strength of the German navy.

To make a kill he would certainly make up for the disappointment of the previous day.

Accordingly 'SALMON' moved in at full speed and by chance the enemy ships turned south and headed straight for her. The submarine turned west to take up a firing position and prepared her salvo of torpedoes. The cruiser 'HIPPER' swung out of station leaving the 'LEIPZIG' in the firing line. At the appropriate moment 'SALMON' fired her 'fish', altered course, and dived deep to avoid the inevitable counter attack. There was a loud explosion while 'SALMON' lay on the bottom and she had a long and nervous wait while depth charges exploded in her vacinity. It was a particularly frightening time for her crew as some of the attackers passed directly overhead.

After what seemed an interminable wait of some hours, the sound of the hunters died away and only then did the boat carefully rise to periscope depth, later surfacing at about 4.30 in the afternoon. Nothing could be seen but a covering of fuel oil spread over an area of about four square miles indicating that 'LEIPZIG' had ended her war in a watery grave.

On returning to her Depôt Ship, the submarine received a rousing welcome; her Commanding Officer, it is said, was promoted to Commander over the heads of 800 other officers and he received the D.S.O. Many of the officers and members of the ships company were also decorated. Winston Churchill was First Lord of the Admiralty at the time and it is thought that the good news brought to him was responsible for the special promotion that Bickford received.

A spectacular patrol had ended with considerable elation, but sadly this was short lived, as on a subsequent operation the valiant boat and her brave crew left her mother ship for the last time, never to return; she is believed to have struck a mine.

The Admiral's grandsons too, shared in the naval life. Humphrey Bickford received encouragement for a taste of the sea and after an education at The Oratory School, Caversham, Reading, he gained entry to the R.N. Engineering College at Keyham near Plymouth.

He appears to have been a clever and diligent student but unfortunately towards the very end of his course, prior to World War II, as an Engineer Sub-Lieutenant, he was involved, with other officers, in a serious motor accident on a Devon country road. He was thrown from the car and on hitting a concrete post one of his thighs was broken. Though the bone was set in hospital it emerged that one leg was shorter than the other and so he was confined to a leg brace for some time. This episode ended his professional naval career - nevertheless his engineering skills were not lost.

During the War years he made a useful contribution with his expertise and worked at the Compass Department of the Admiralty. Those who knew him remarked on his agility as he was seen clambering over submarine casements in spite of his 'dicky leg'. His skills were amply demonstrated and with knowledge and ability for design he invented a gadget for use with compasses mainly in submarines which was known as 'The Bickford Non-sparking Relay'.

Some years after the War his life ended prematurely in Malaya after being struck down by an attack of Poliomiolitis which he contracted there.

His brother, Cyprian, another grandson, also joined the Service and entered the Royal Naval College, Dartmouth at the age of thirteen by way of competitive examination. He remained there as a cadet before joining the cruiser H.M.S. NEPTUNE in South Africa, early in the War, as a midshipman.

The ship was involved in the Battle of Calabria, off Italy, and had the distinction of being the first ship of a British Naval Force to sight the enemy fleet in the Mediterranean since the Napoleonic Wars.

Then, having seen service in a number of other overseas theatres of War, in surface ships of various kinds, he returned home, as a Sub-Lieutenant, and was encouraged to volunteer for the Submarine Service; he was advised that it might enhance his career prospects. As a submariner he experienced many exciting and hazardous operations. After having been promoted to Lieutenant, he operated further afield on patrols in Japanese controlled waters off Malasia.

Following the end of hostilities the call of dry land proved too strong and he decided upon a different career. This was a common occurrence and not surprising as many young men had been thrust into the Navy to experience the horrors of War at an early age.

Meantime the line of Naval service has been carried on by the Admiral's great grand-daughter, and the authors daughter, Bernadette, who completed her spell of service with the London Division of the Royal Naval Reserve, as a Wren writer, on board H.M.S. PRESIDENT, moored on the Thames at Victoria Embankment.

Her sea time consisted of a stormy trip to the Channel Islands in the Divisional mine sweeper H.M.S. GLASSERTON. Ashore, apart from evening drills and training, there were additional assignments such as being delivered to a wild spot on Dartmoor with other Wrens and sailors and then being told to find their way home. It was said to be a test of initiative and of survival skills but equally likely was it in preparation for their forthcoming march in the procession of the Lord Mayor's Show.

Those days are now passed and it seems that with the reduction in numbers of naval personnel fewer ladies than hitherto will be required to assist in the work of the Service; a great sadness for many.

Today, we live in an uncertain world with altering tasks for the Royal Navy. Many of those who follow in the Admiral's footsteps are unsure of what the future holds when naval careers are often cut short in their prime as a result of financial constraints imposed by Government.

In addition, a new breed of sailor seems to be needed at a time when ships are few and ever changing, both in construction and operation. Technology seems to have taken over from the many human skills formerly employed in fighting ships.

The Royal Navy generally appears to be heading for a role which concerns a rather different set of activities such as Fishery protection, Rescue, and special operations on behalf of the Oil Industry. This will, necessarily, result in a reduced need for the wider duty of policing the oceans of the world which it undertook in the days of the Empire. However these new requirements are not really so very different from times past when 'PEGASUS' and 'KATOOMBA' were likewise performing special missions on behalf of the Nation.

APPENDIX I

OWNERS OF DUNSLAND HOUSE

John Cadiho	(1086)
The house is said to have remained for 8 generations in the Cadiho Family	
Thomazin Cadiho (niece) m. John Dabernon	d. 1425
Sir John Dabernon (son)	d. 1432
Elizabeth Dabernon (daughter) m. William Battyn	
Robert Battyn (son)	
Humphry Battyn (son)	d. 1522
Philippa Battyn (daughter) m. John Arscott	
Humphry Arscott (son)	d. 1580
John Arscott (son)	d. 1623
Arthur Arscott (son)	d. 1662
Grace Arscott (daughter) m. William Bickford	d. 1686
Arscott Bickford (son)	d. 1693
William Bickford (son)	d. 1740
Arscott Bickford (son)	d.s.p. 1771
George Bickford (brother)	d. 1795
Arscott Bickford (son)	d. 1817
Mary Bickford (sister) m. William Holland Coham	d. 1839
William Bickford Coham (son)	d. 1843
William Holland Bickford Coham (son)	d. 1880
Augusta Christiana Davie Coham(sister) m. Harvey Dickenson	d. 1901
Arscott William Harvey Dickinson (son) sold Estate to The National Trust in 1945	
House destroyed by fire	1967

APPENDIX II

THE VISITATIONS OF THE COUNTY OF DEVON.

a

Marye, bap. 6 Jan. 1600-1 at Bradford,[2] *ætat. 20, 1620*, died s.p.

William Bickford of Bickford Town in the parish of Plympton St. Mary, bur. 3 Nov. 1659 at Bradford.[2] M.I. Will 13 Ap. 1659, pro. 5 Dec. 1660 P.C.C. (Nabbs 261). = *Grace 2 fil. ætat. 19*, 1620, eventually the heiress of this line, mar. 9 Dec 1634 at Bradford,[2] named in her husband's will, bur. 13 Jan. 1686-7 at Bradford.[2] M.I.

Bridget, da. of Edmond Prideaux, 3 wife, mar. 8 July 1683 at Padstow[1] bur. 18 June 1712 at Bradford.[2] = Honor, da. of John Prideaux, 2 wife. = Arscott Bickford, sole exr. of his father's will, bur. 19 June 1693 at Bradford,[2] = Mary, da. of Edmund Parker, mar. 27 Dec. 1660 at Plympton St. Mary,[3] bur. 1 Sep. 1675 at Bradford.[2]

Mary, bur. 20 Mar. 1635-6 at Bradford.[2]

Frances, bap. 29 Nov. 1637 at Bradford.[2]

Elizabeth, bap. 26 June 1639 at Bradford,[2] mar. ... Rowland, named in her father's will, living 1659.

William Harris = Honor, bap. 14 Nov. 1679, mar. 12 Feb. 1699-1700 at Bradford.[2]

Edward Bickford, bur. 30 Sep. 1677 at Bradford.[2]

Bridget, bap. 13 Feb. 1690-1, bur. 1 Jan. 1693-4 at Bradford.[2]

Nicholas Bickford, bap. 23 Oct. 1689, bur. 31 July 1690 at Bradford[2]

Edmond Bickford, 2 son, bap. 21 October 1685 at Bradford.[2]

Arscott Bickford, bur. 19 February 1695-6 at Bradford.[2]

Arscott Bickford, bur. 22 May 1686 at Bradford.[2]

Elizabeth, da. of the Rev. John Richards, Rector of Bradford, 3 wife, married 7 Nov. 1733 at Bradford.[2] = Damaris, da. and heir of Edward Hoblyn of Nanswhyden, mar. 14 May 1712, 2 wife, bur. 26 July 1729 at Bradford.[2] = William Bickford, eldest son and heir, bap. 2 Sep. 1684, bur. 26 Feb. 1740-1 at Bradford.[2] = Bridget, da. of Edmund Tremayne, bap. 21 Oct. 1684 at Lamerton,[4] mar. 12 Nov. 1707 at Maristow,[5] bur. 11 Feb. 1708-9 at Bradford.[2]

George Bickford, only son, and heir to his half brother Arscott Bickford and exr. of his will, bur. 27 May 1795 at Bradford.[2] = Mary, da. of *, bur. 10 Nov. 1803 at Bradford.[2]

Damaris, bap. 23 May 1716, bur. 22 May 1717 at Bradford.[2]

Edward Bickford, died an infant, bap. 25 Jan. 1714-15, died 16, bur. 21 Jan. 1715-16 at Bradford.[2]

Arscott Bickford of Okehampton, bap. 5 Feb. 1712-13 at Bradford,[2] residuary legatee and sole exr. of the will of his brother William,[8] bur. 26 Ap. 1771 at Bradford.[2]

Bridget, bap. 9 Dec. 1763 at Okehampton.[6]

Elizabeth, bap. 14 Oct. 1773 at Cookbury,[7] died s.p. 21 January 1820. Will without date, pro. 25 Feb. 1820 P.C.C.

Arscott Bickford, "born and bap. at Okehampton, received into the Church" the same day his sister Elizabeth was baptized, 14 Oct. 1773 at Cookbury,[7] bur. 25 July 1817 at Bradford,[2] s.p., æt. 48.

William Bickford, Clerk in Holy Orders, bap. 12 June 1717, bur. 30 May 1746 at Bradford.[2] Will 4 Apl. 1745.[8]

Edward Bickford, bap. 25 Aug. 1718, bur. 12 July 1743 at Bradford.[2]

The Rev. William Holland Coham of Coham, co. Devon, Rector of Halwill and J.P., died 15 March 1825 at Coham, æt. 61. = Mary, 3 da., and eventually heiress of this family, bap 2 May 1767 at Okehampton,[6] mar. 29 Nov. 1790 at Bradford,[2] died 4 Feb. 1839.

Mary Anne, bap. 20 Ap. 1793 at Bradford.[2]

Christian, bap. 25 June 1785 at Bradford,[2] extrix. of the will of her aunt Elizabeth Bickford,[8] married to George Boughton Kingdon, and died s.p.

Holland Coham, 4 son, bap. 2 Ap. 1804 at Bradford,[2] Clerk in Holy Orders and J.P., died unmar. 26 Mar. 1867, æt. 62.

George Lewis Coham, 1 son.

Stephen Coham, 3 son, bap. 7 Mar. 1797 at Bradford,[2] a Midshipman H.M.S. Severn, drowned at Deal 23 Oct. 1819.

The Rev. William Bickford Coham of Coham, 2 son, bap. 6 Ap. 1792 at Bradford,[2] died 2 July 1843. = Augusta Mary Davie, eldest da. of Joseph Davie Basset of Watermouth, mar. 17 Ap. 1837 at Berrynarbor.[9]

William Holland Bickford Coham, 1 son, b. 28 July 1828, J.P. and D.L. = Dora Elizabeth Louisa, da. of Sir Hopton Stratford Scott, K.C.B., of Woodville, near Lucan, Dublin, mar. 3 Sep. 1857.

Arscott Bickford Courtenay Coham, 2 son, born 29 Ap. 1832, died unmar.

Elinor Mary Bassett, mar. 17 Aug. 1852 to William Parr of Fernside, Bournemouth, co. Dorset.

Augusta Christiana Davie, mar. Ap. 1858 to Captain Harvey George Dickinson, Madras Army.

Elinor Mary Bickford.

---

1 Padstow, Cornwall, Parish Register.
2 Bradford Parish Register.
3 Plympton St. Mary Parish Register.
4 [illegible]erton Parish Register.
5 [illegible]stow Parish Register.
6 Okehampton Parish Register.
7 Cookbury Parish Register.
8 Charity Commissioners Report, 1824, vol. xiv.
9 Berrynarbor Parish Register.

1 Harl. MS. 1080.
2 Harl. MS. 1163, fo. 176.
4 Robert Arscott, Harl. MS. 11[illegible]
5 Richard Arscott, Harl. MS. 116o,

* J. PALFREMAN

(With permission of the Devon West Central Library, Plymouth)

APPENDIX III

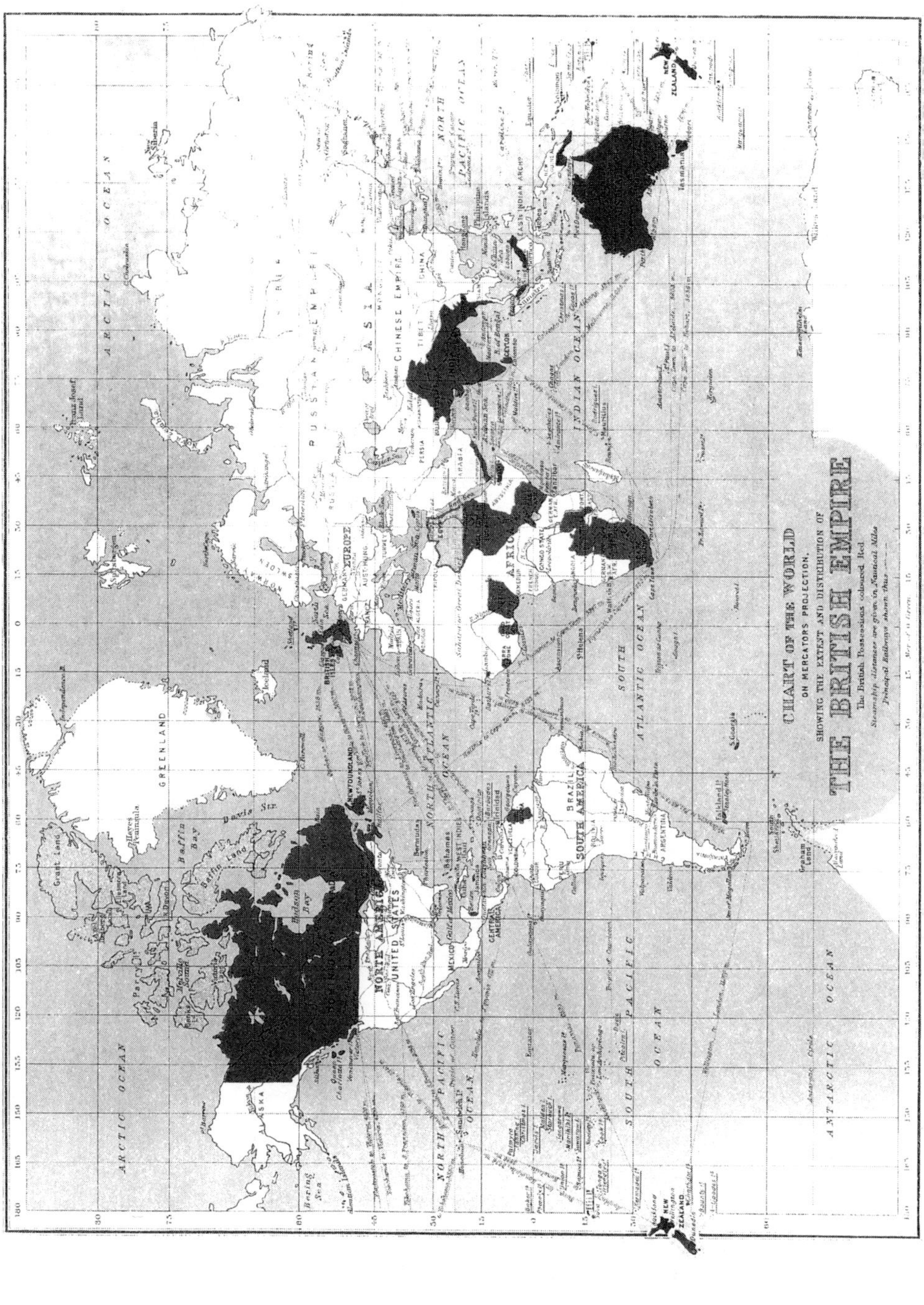

APPENDIX IV

William Bickford (1755 – 1822) = Ann Darley (1766 – 1836, m. 1781)

William Kennedy (c. 1765)

Joseph Bickford (1781 – 1859) = Louisa Maria Tomlin (b. 1786, m. 1812)

Captain Kennedy R.N. (1787 – 1854) = Maria Pinnock (m.c. 1833)

William Bickford (1813 – 1846) = Maria Pinnock Kennedy (1820 – 1846, m. 1841)

Admiral A.K. Bickford C.M.G. (1844 – 1927) = Kathleen Louise Dore (1850 – 1910)

Andrew	Arther	Marie	John	Winifride	Maurice	Francis
b. 1869	b. 1870	b. 1875	b. 1879	b. 1886	b. 1888	b. 1889

Pedigree of
Admiral A. K. Bickford C.M.G.

APPENDIX V

N
COLE ISLAND
MAGAZINE
ESQUIMALT
RLY
RLY JETTY
ADMIRALS ROAD
HUDSON BAY PROPERTY
LEVEL CROSSING
LIMIT OF R.N. ANCHORAGE
RN HOSPITAL
ESQUIMALT HARBOUR
BICKFORD TOWER ON GRANT KNOLL
DOCK
R.N COAL WHARF
R.N DOCKYARD
VILLAGE
R.N MINING WHARF
RN RECREATION GROUND
OLD ROAD
FISGUARD LIGHT
RIFLE RANGE
ROAD TO VICTORIA FROM DOCKYARD
SIGNAL HILL
BROTHERS ISLAND
ESQUIMALT NAVAL BASE 1902 (SKETCH PLAN)
R.F.B

BIBLIOGRAPHY

"A Footnote to History" by Robert Louis Stevenson.

"My Naval Career 1880-1928" by Admiral Sir Sydney Fremantle G.C.B. MVO.

"The Navy I have Known" by Admiral Hon Sir Edmund Fremantle G.C.B G.C.V.O. C.M.G.

"The Naval side of British History" by Sir Geoffrey Callender M.A. FSA.

"The Commission of H.M.S. GRAFTON 1902-1905" by Albert Newton A.B.

"The Royal Navy and the Northwest Coast of North America 1810-1914" by Professor Barry Gough.

"Esquimalt Naval Base" - A History of its Work and its Defences by Major F.V. Longhurst 1941.

"The Daily Colonist" Victoria B.C. Canada October 2nd 1901

"Up Periscope" by David Masters 1942

DOCUMENTARY REFERENCES

Admiral Andrew Kennedy BICKFORD C.M.G.

Published & Unpublished Sources

This list indicates only those documents which have yielded information, it does not reflect all the files/books that have been examined.

Public Records Office, Kew

Unpublished Sources:

ADM 1	5876 - 5877	In letters, Commander in Chief S. China	
ADM 1	6412	Letters, Commander in Chief 'Brazils'	
ADM 1	6713	Letters, Commander in Chief China	
ADM 1	7154	Letters, Commander in Chief Australia	
ADM 1	7176	Captains [B] letters	
ADM 12	1114	Captains [B] letters	
ADM 12	1119	Captains [B] letters	
ADM 12	1130	Admiralty Digest 1885	
ADM 12	1146	Admiralty Digest 1886	
ADM 12	1194	Letters, Commander in Chief Portsmouth	
ADM 12	1210	Captains [B] letters 1890	
ADM 12	1213	Captains [M] letters 1890	
ADM 12	1247	Captains [B] letters 1893	
ADM 12	1250	Captains [K] letters 1893	
ADM 50	360	Admirals Journals, Pacific Station	
ADM 53	8696 - 8697	Log H.M.S. BARROSA	1863 to 1865
ADM 53	9068	Log H.M.S. RESEARCH	1865 to 1867
ADM 53	10881 - 10882	Log H.M.S. AMETHYST	1876 to 1878
ADM 53	12567 - 12571	Log H.M.S. ASSISTANCE	1887 to 1889
ADM 53	14234	Log H.M.S. KATOOMBA	1892 to 1894
ADM 53	14496	Log H.M.S. MEDUSA	1890

ADM 53	14905 - 14906	Log H.M.S. PEGASUS	1883 to 1885
ADM 53	16567	Log H.M.S. WARSPITE	1902
ADM116	33	Admiralty papers, Egyptian Operations	
ADM155	1	Index of Correspondence	
ADM196	36 part 1	Certificates of Service	
ADM196	40	Certificates of Service	

Published Sources:

Lloyd's Register of Shipping 1882/83
Navy List, various dates
Annual Register (Parliamentary Papers) 1863 - 1865
Royal United Service Institute Journal
Army & Navy Illustrated
Conways All The Worlds Ships 1860 - 1905
British Battleships - Oscar Parkes

INDEX